sensing
the rhythm

finding my voice in a world without sound

mandy harvey
and mark atteberry

HOWARD BOOKS
AN IMPRINT OF SIMON & SCHUSTER, INC.

new york   london   toronto   sydney   new delhi

Howard Books
An Imprint of Simon & Schuster, Inc.
1230 Avenue of the Americas
New York, NY 10020

Copyright © 2017 by Mandy Harvey and Mark Atteberry

First Howard Books hardcover edition September 2017

HOWARD and colophon are trademarks of Simon & Schuster, Inc.

For information about special discounts for bulk purchases, please contact Simon & Schuster Special Sales at 1-866-506-1949 or business@simonandschuster.com.

The Simon & Schuster Speakers Bureau can bring authors to your live event. For more information or to book an event, contact the Simon & Schuster Speakers Bureau at 1-866-248-3049 or visit our website at www.simonspeakers.com.

Interior design by Davina Mock-Maniscalco
Images of music notes and microphone copyright © Shutterstock

Manufactured in the United States of America

10   9   8   7   6   5   4   3   2   1

Library of Congress Cataloging-in-Publication Data is available.

ISBN 978-1-5011-7225-0
ISBN 978-1-5011-7227-4 (ebook)

for everyone who's feeling tempted to give up.
may this book give you hope and the courage to keep moving forward.

contents

contents

a thing to behold

I'm standing in the wings, waiting to go on.

My band members are milling around, bantering in the casual way that accomplished musicians who are fully confident in their abilities tend to do. There's not a jangled nerve among them, but there's plenty of urgency, like tethered falcons hungry for the hunt. Once they settle behind their instruments, I will sever their bonds with a downbeat and watch them take flight.

It is a thing to behold, this unleashing of talent that fills a room with music the way water fills a submerged pitcher. Shoulders hunch, heads bob, brows wrinkle, fingers dance, all with a symmetry that could no more be prevented than it could be planned. The people in the audience will respond enthusiastically, of course, for they have not ended up here by circling the wrong date on their calendars or taking the wrong exit off the roundabout. They have come to witness the un-leashing and to experience the filling.

Yes, it is quite a thing to behold.

It is no doubt quite a thing to hear, too, but I'll have to take your word for that because tonight, once again, I will sing with my amaz-ing musicians, everything from sultry ballads to blistering jazz, with-out hearing a single note.

Sound impossible?

It does to me, too.

I lost my hearing when I was nineteen. It happened over a period of a few months, leaving me profoundly deaf, which, by the way, is the official term for people who are unable to hear any sound below ninety-five decibels in their better ear. The less tactful among us might say that I'm "stone deaf" or "deaf as a post." I just know that to-night I won't hear what everyone else does.

When I walk onstage, I won't hear the master of ceremonies say, "Ladies and gentlemen, would you please welcome Mandy Harvey!"

When my band kicks off the first tune, I won't hear that amazing chord substitution my piano player throws in or the clever lick my sax player answers with.

When I finish the first tune, I will see the people clapping, but I won't hear their applause.

Most people wonder how it's possible for me to be an award-winning professional musician with such a drastic limitation.

How can I sing on pitch without hearing the notes?

How can I stay on beat without hearing the drums and bass?

How can I learn other composers' songs when I can't hear them?

How can I write my own songs without the ability to hear the notes and chords I have to choose from?

And, most of all, how did I keep from losing my mind, not to mention my faith, when, as a college music major dreaming of a career in music, my hearing started slowly and irrevocably slipping away?

I decided to write this book not just to answer these questions, but because the twisting, rocky, uphill road I've been on for the last ten years has given me some life-changing insights, some lessons that I feel are worth sharing.

I can't tell you *why* I experienced the loss I have or even why I'm able to do what I do. I certainly never wanted to be that girl everyone hears about and says, "Wow, *that's* weird!" But I must admit: this road, while excruciatingly hard at times, has opened my eyes to truths and realities that a lifetime of study and lectures would never have taught me. The result is that, even minus my hearing, I am a more complete person than I have ever been. Not perfect, as

Even minus my hearing, I am a more complete person than I have ever been.

you will see, but farther along the road toward my potential than I would have been without the challenges I have faced.

As I tell you my story, my goal is to share the most pertinent of these life lessons with you in the hope that one or more of them might be just what you need to hear at a critical moment in your life. I promise not to bore you with a tedious chronology of everything that's happened to me, but rather to show you some snapshots of those extraordinary moments when pain and truth collided, causing light and understanding to rain down around me. Perhaps what I share will help you in the way I have been helped.

And so, at the end of each chapter, I've included a page titled "Making Sense of *YOUR* Rhythm," which summarizes the lessons in that chapter. It is my hope and prayer that the lessons I've learned along the way will give you hope—and maybe a little guidance—as you find your own unique and beautiful rhythm.

John Wooden, the legendary basketball coach, once said, "Things turn out best for people who make the best of the way things turn out."[1] If this book, in some small way, helps you make the best of the way things have turned out in your life, it will have been worth it all.

Blessed are the piecemakers.

—sign in a quilt shop

one

you reap what you *sew*

$\mathcal{I}$ was a first-semester freshman at Colorado State University. I should have been filled with the excitement of taking on a new challenge, making new friends, and finally starting to chase my dream. But something was wrong with me, and living in denial just wasn't working anymore. Trips to the doctor had revealed that I had lost forty decibels of hearing in both ears. Unless my hearing free fall suddenly stopped, which I knew wasn't likely, I would soon be deaf.

Such a realization would be hard for anyone to process, of course, but it was particularly devastating to me because of my passion for music. As kids we close our eyes and see ourselves as adults, doing amazing and wonderful things. Every dream I'd ever had growing up was somehow connected to music. I desperately needed my ears to cooperate, and they wouldn't. At first I was worried, but as things continued to deteriorate, I started losing it. I was falling apart.

Back home, my sister Katie was married, my other sister Sammi was a junior in high school, and my brother, Josh, was just starting high school. They were wrapped up in adventures of their own. My parents, too, had a lot going on in their lives. My mother was working for a rheumatology practice and my father was busy on the ministry staff at our church. Of course, my parents were fully aware that something was going on with me, but because of the distance, they had no idea how fragile my emotional state had become. One day my intuitive mother suggested that my dad drive to the campus and spend some time with me. He didn't have a car available, so he borrowed a church van and made the trip from Longmont to Fort Collins. When he pulled up, I was waiting for him in the parking lot.

I'll never forget our conversation. I was desperate to make sense out of what was happening, to understand why God would give me such a wonderful talent and then allow my hearing—the sense I would need more than any other—to slip away. But as we all know, answers to such questions are not easy to come by. People have been asking the *why* question since the beginning of time, often to no avail. Sitting in the van that day, we too came to that same brick wall. I remember Dad saying, "You don't have to look for some master plan here, just stay on the path of faith."

But understanding why this was happening wasn't my only issue.

I was losing things one by one—important, precious things—and my heart was breaking. I had even started carrying a small notebook so I could write down things I could no longer hear. The list was growing frighteningly long.

As Dad and I sat together in the van, I felt a sudden and powerful emotional shift. We had been talking about big-picture issues like my classes and what the future might hold for my education, when suddenly I began weeping. Dad asked me what was wrong. It was then that I confessed something that I had been keeping to myself, but that had been torturing my soul: I couldn't remember what his voice sounded like. "I see your mouth move. I know what you're saying. But in my head I hear your words in *my* voice, not yours."

"I see your mouth move. I know what you're saying. But in my head I hear your words in *my* voice, not yours."

My dad says that at that moment the breath went out of him and sorrow such as he'd never known swept over him like a gigantic wave. We both felt that something priceless had been stolen from us. Imagine not being able to remember the sound of a loved one's voice. Or, if you were in my dad's place, realizing that your daughter would never again be able to hear your words of encouragement, your singing, your silly jokes, or your laughter. I'm sure you've had a moment when you just needed to hear a special loved one's voice. Sometimes nothing in the world feels as good. But I would never again hear the voice I had loved and trusted.

Suddenly, there was nothing more for either of us to say. We sat there in the van and hugged and cried and prayed. My dad still says that was the moment when he fully understood that nothing would ever be the same.

Growing up, I had had problems with my ears. "Deformed Eustachian tubes" was the official diagnosis. In practical terms, I had a hard time getting the pressure inside my head to match the pressure out-side my head. I often felt like you feel when you're at a high altitude and your ears need to pop, except that my ears wouldn't pop. That un-relieved pressure caused my eardrums to perforate more times than I can count and caused me to score below normal on school hearing tests. At times I felt lost in conversations if people mumbled or looked away from me while talking. So yes, there were times when, because of all the ear problems, I thought about what it would be like to lose my hearing. Still, when you're starting college and stacking one new experience on top of another, when the dream you've carried in your heart since childhood finally appears to be within reach, you don't think your ears are just going to start shutting down.

But I don't want anyone's pity. Lots of people have suffered way more than I have. I may have lost my hearing, but I've been blessed with a wonderful family and countless friends. I've had an incredi-ble career in music, recorded albums, performed in legendary venues, been in commercials, and written a book. My life, like everyone's, is a mixture of good and bad. A patchwork.

Which reminds me of my grandmother, Lyndall Watson. Grand-mama is eighty-one years old as I write these words and still a blessing to all who know her. Like most women her age, she possesses skills and abilities that have pretty much gone the way of the 8-track tape—like sewing, for example.

For years she made clothes and curtains and quilts for our entire family; no telling how much money she saved us. Virtually all the blankets in my house to this day are quilts that she made. My favorite is one she made from scraps she saved from all the dresses she made for me throughout my childhood. When I look at that quilt, all kinds of precious memories flash through my mind. It saddens me to think that my generation may be the last one to receive such amazing gifts.

When I picture Grandmama working on one of her quilts, I can't help thinking about how a life is made. There are all kinds of metaphors I'm sure you've heard, like life being a story you write or a journey you make or a mountain you climb. But to me, life is the art of sewing together countless pieces—responsibilities, experiences, blessings, hardships, relationships, and challenges—to make something that is, in the end, both meaningful to oneself and beneficial to others.

Life is the art of sewing together countless pieces to make something that is, in the end, both meaningful and beneficial.

It's not easy.

The biggest problem we face in trying to stitch together a life is that we're often handed an ugly piece we don't like, never wanted, and wish we could get rid of . . . but we can't. In my case, it was hearing loss. But I also think about that struggling single mom whose husband left her for another woman. Or that grieving parent whose teenage son or daughter was killed by a drunk driver. Or the countless wounded warriors who sign up to protect our freedoms and come home profoundly changed in painful ways.

Perhaps you, even as you read these words, are doing battle with a hardship that seems cruelly unfair. Because of my work with No Barriers USA, I meet a lot of people who have been handed circumstances they never would have chosen and certainly would have declined if given the option. Many of them are living extraordinary lives that are rich in significance, but a good many are still trying to make sense of that ugly piece of life they've been handed, recoiling at its unseemly appearance and rejecting any notion that it could ever add something meaningful to their lives.

Because the truth is, hardships always feel like a subtraction. Our first thought when something bad happens is of what we're in danger of losing. We're bereft, sometimes stunned, and completely unable to see any potential for good. That's what my dad and I were wrestling with that day in the van. As my dad and I wept in each other's arms, there's no way you could have convinced me that I wasn't facing massive subtractions from my life that would ultimately diminish me as a person and ruin all my hopes and dreams.

Even if I hadn't found a way to live out my passion for music, my hearing loss would likely still have been a net plus in my life.

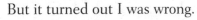

But it turned out I was wrong.

Yes, there have been subtractions, but there have also been significant additions.

Losing my hearing has taught me things about myself I never knew and might never have learned. It has also led me to some amazing people and experiences that I likely would not have encountered otherwise. Even my dream of a life in music, which at one point seemed to have vanished like a vapor, has returned to me in proportions I never would have thought possible. But even if that hadn't happened, my hearing loss would likely still have been a net plus in my life, simply by making me more thoughtful and compassionate and patient toward others, or by putting me in a position to be an encouragement to someone in need.

Countless others have also found additions in their hardships.

When Christopher Reeve, the world-famous actor, suddenly became a quadriplegic as the result of a spinal cord injury he suffered during an equestrian accident, the whole world saw it as the cruelest subtraction of all. And why not? How could anything worse possibly happen to a person? But history shows that it was when Reeve lost the ability to be active that he became one of the world's greatest activists. His lobbying and fund-raising efforts funneled millions of dollars into spinal cord injury research and brought hope to people who thought they'd never have any ever again. His final book, *Nothing Is Impossible*, doesn't sound like the treatise of a man who saw his life in terms of subtractions, does it?

Yes, history presents us with an unending parade of people whose hardships *added* more to their lives than they would have ever thought possible. This is why you must never be afraid to take the ugly pieces you're handed—the disabilities, the disappointments, the failures, the betrayals—and sew them in among the pretty pieces of your life.

What, specifically, does that mean?

For one thing, it means not living in denial. Pretending you don't have a problem only allows the problem to grow bigger while at the same time diminishing you in the eyes of others.

It also means not growing bitter. Living in bitterness is the opposite of living in denial. It's when you wear your hardship on your sleeve and make sure everyone you meet knows how ticked off you are about it.

Finally, and above all, it means not giving up. This is really the heart of the matter. Sewing together a life means you go on, embracing whatever reality you find yourself in.

Whether you like what's happening, or not.

Whether you can make sense of it, or not.

Whether you think you can meet the challenges ahead, or not.

You crawl out of bed every day and handle whatever is in front of you to the best of your ability and let the results take care of themselves.

Somebody said that the hardest thing about life is that it's so daily. I'm sure it was someone who'd been handed a hardship. When you're hurting or scared or confused, just making it through another twenty-four-hour period can seem like an impossible task. But when all is said and done, this is how you piece together a life. This is how you find additions to offset, and even overwhelm, your subtractions: by getting up every day and going on in spite of everything.

And make no mistake: this stitching together of the blessings and hardships you are handed never ends. I've already got quite a life-quilt going, but I'm only twenty-nine years old. If I live a normal life span, I know I'll be given many more pieces. Some might even be uglier than what I've already received. I plan to be "sewing" for the rest of my life.

Let me take you back to my favorite quilt, the one Grandmama made out of pieces of all the dresses she made for me when I was a child. As you might imagine, it's not the most beautiful quilt in the world. The fabric squares are quite a conglomeration, a riot of clashing colors and patterns that would surely relegate it to a spot on the half-price table of a fancy quilt shop.

But to me, it's the most beautiful quilt ever made.

And to anyone who understands what the squares represent, it's perfect, which should be a reminder to us all that it's not the aesthetics of its individual pieces that make a quilt or a life beautiful. It's the significance each piece holds, and the care and patience with which they were sewn together.

making sense of **YOUR** *rhythm*

Mingle the "ugly" pieces of your life quilt with the "pretty" ones:

- ✦ Refuse to live in denial.

- ✦ Don't allow yourself to grow bitter.

- ✦ Never, ever give up.

Closing Encouragement

It's not the aesthetics of individual pieces that make a quilt or a life beautiful. It's the significance each piece holds and the care and patience with which they were sewn together.

No matter how hard we try,
no matter how clever our plan,
we cannot arrange for the life we desire.[2]

—John Eldredge

two

no dream is immortal

*W*hen I enrolled at Colorado State University to start pursuing my goal of becoming a music teacher, I was as happy as I'd ever been. It appeared that the tributaries of passion, talent, and opportunity had all merged to form a raging river that would carry me to the fulfillment of my dream. I closed my eyes and saw myself just a few years in the future, standing before a high school choir, the students' eyes glued to me, their mouths open wide, their faces red with effort, their neck veins about to burst. I saw them responding to my every wink and gesture, filling the hall with rapturous music. I saw their parents smiling—no, make that *glowing*—amazed at what their teenagers—these strange creatures who found it so difficult to make a bed or empty a trash can—were able to accomplish together. Simply put, I saw myself as all young dreamers do, living the perfect life.

A mere seven months later, that dream was a cold, stiff corpse.

Let me tell you about the funeral.

The funeral was in May, right at the end of my freshman year at CSU. No, it didn't involve a gathering of solemn-faced family and friends, all dressed in black, at a church or funeral home. Rather, it happened at the university in the organ recital hall, at what should have been the happiest occasion of the year: the music department's freshman voice recital, an annual event that gives the students a chance to show their families and loved ones the progress they've made (and to make their parents feel better about the money they've invested).

My classmates and friends had indeed made progress. Breathtakingly so, in some cases. I, on the other hand, was a different story. I had spent almost the entire year losing my hearing and sinking into a pit of despair.

A little history: about a month into my fall semester, I noticed I was having trouble hearing my psychology professor. At first, I chalked it up to her speaking too softly and me sitting too far back in the room. I even told myself that the girl sitting next to me must not be able to hear the teacher either because she always seemed distracted. (I didn't want to consider that maybe she was just a disinterested student.)

Before long, my rationalizations began to wilt under the increasingly hot sun of reality. There simply was no denying that something was going on with my ears. I went to the doctor, and, sure enough, he found that I had lost about thirty decibels of hearing. He scheduled another test for a few weeks later. That one revealed a hearing loss of fifty-five decibels, which is just five decibels short of being legally deaf.

As the holidays rolled in that year, I was in a bad place emotionally, but I clung to a glimmer of hope: *my doctor had ordered hearing aids*. I prayed they would be the game changer that would resuscitate my limping, wheezing dream.

When the hearing aids came in, I was thrilled to find that they helped.

Unfortunately, they only helped for about two weeks.

The thing about hearing aids is that they only amplify the hearing you have. In other words, if you've lost certain frequencies, they can't give you those back. They can only work with the frequencies you have left, which essentially means that they're just making your lousy hearing louder. This is why people who have hearing aids often don't wear them. Their family members get frustrated, asking, "Why aren't you wearing your hearing aids? We spent so much money on them!" But amplified bad hearing is not what a hearing-impaired person needs.

To my utter horror, my hearing continued to deteriorate to the point that the hearing aids were useless. By the end of February, I had passed the point of being legally deaf and became what's called "profoundly deaf."

I know what you're thinking.

You're wondering why I was still in

By the end of February, I had passed the point of being legally deaf and became what's called "profoundly deaf."

school. If I couldn't hear, how could I function as a music major? And why would I want to try? I certainly would never be able to help young singers if I couldn't hear what they sounded like. Why didn't I just give up and go home?

I've been asked this question many times. Part of the answer is that I have a stubborn streak. I've never been one to give up easily. But even more relevant is the fact that, at that point, I was determined to hang on to anything I could possibly hang on to for as long as I could. So many things that I loved were no longer mine, and in their place were changes I didn't want. I desperately wanted to cling to one thing, to control one decision, and so I kept showing up for class, pretending I could hear, pretending that my dream could still come true.

And so we come to the year-end freshman voice recital, the ultimate and inevitable result of my refusal to drop out of school. In a season of life that presented me with many bad days, that one may have been the worst of all.

First, I was totally unable to haul myself out of bed to even go to the venue. I was in a state of full-blown depression, but even more debilitating in that moment was the certainty that what awaited me at the recital was a mortifying disaster. I knew I would be surrounded by terrifically talented people singing difficult pieces, most of them in Italian, French, and German. I, at one time, could have done the same. But now, with most of my hearing gone, I had planned to sing a simple spiritual, "Deep River," a song that took no vocal chops whatsoever—a song that was as out of place on the program as a tank top in a room full of wedding dresses.

Somehow, about twenty minutes before the recital was to start,

I managed to crawl out of bed. I didn't have time to shower or put on makeup. I put my hair in a half ponytail and threw on an old dress that I had worn in a high school musical that featured music from the 1940s. Even it was out of place.

I didn't have time to shower or put on makeup. I put my hair in a half ponytail and threw on an old dress that I had worn in a high school musical.

When I arrived at the hall, teachers and students politely gave me pity smiles and quickly looked at the floor. I didn't blame them. They sensed as well as I did that I was making a big mistake. And yes, even then I could have simply walked out the door and gone home. Perhaps I should have.

Then, as if some cosmic evil force was toying with me the way a cat bats around a wounded mouse, I saw that I was one of the last singers on the program.

Let that sink in.

By the time my turn came, the people would have sat through one amazing performance after another. The pieces for the recital had been chosen for their difficulty, and the students, many of whom were truly gifted, had been practicing for months. You can imagine the uneasy feeling that fell over the room as I got up to sing. My classmates' family members and friends had some basic understanding of what I'd been going through, and surely wondered what I was doing on the program. My own family sat in the audience, not fully aware of how badly I'd been doing the last several weeks. I know everyone felt a sense of foreboding, believing that what they were about to witness couldn't possibly go well.

It didn't.

I stood by the piano, close enough so that I could put my hand on it and feel the vibrations, which would at least help me feel the time. When my accompanist finished the introduction, I froze, unable to remember the first word of the song. Suddenly, my eyes filled with tears, and an urge to flee the room swallowed me up. But I had begun and didn't know how to stop. Weeping from start to finish, I doggedly pushed through and finished the song. My "performance" became even more humiliating when my classmates and teachers gave me "deaf applause," which is when you hold your hands head-high and waggle them. Others saw this and joined in. Soon the entire audience was waggling their hands in the air.

Backstage, none of my classmates spoke to me. When I came into their view, they'd find something or someone to distract them. I don't blame them. I'm sure they had no idea what to say. In their shoes, I wouldn't have known what to say either. And saying nothing is always better than saying something that would only deepen someone's pain.

When our family got home, it really was as if we had just returned from a funeral. There was that I'm-glad-it's-over sense of relief, along with the somber realization that something once cherished was gone from our midst forever. The house seemed a little emptier, similar to the feeling when there's suddenly an empty seat at the table.

Just one year prior, I had been selected the top female vocalist at my high school. I had flown to Australia with an all-star high school choir to sing at the Sydney Opera House. I had been accepted into the university of my choice. And now I was done. An event that for the other students had been a celebration of hard work and accomplishment was, for me, the official public confirmation that my dream was dead, that my friends would be moving on without me, that I would have to find something else to do with my life.

That recital was the official public confirmation that my dream was dead and that I would have to find something else to do with my life.

That's when I learned that no dream is immortal.

Sometimes, when I hear a motivational speaker urging people never to give up on their dreams, I want to say, "Excuse me, but what if your dream gives up on you? What if your dream is to be a music teacher and you lose your hearing? What if your dream is to be a professional athlete and you become paralyzed? What if your dream is to be a model and your face is disfigured in an accident?"

Oh, how easy it is to be all Pollyanna-ish when talking about dreams. My dad calls this "the theology of the healthy." It's the highly naïve notion (that mostly healthy, successful people have) that if you just do *your* part, fate will do *its* part and everyone will live happily ever after.

How I wish this were always true, but I am living proof that it isn't. And I'm not the only one.

Which brings me to a pretty important question: What do you do when your dream dies? What do you do when life steps up and smacks you down and then waggles a finger in your face?

When my hearing first started to fade, I fought the possibility that the end of my dream might be in sight. But eventually, I had to face the truth, and the lessons I learned during that process might be helpful to you as well.

The first thing you have to do is make sure your dream really is dead.

We've all heard stories about unconscious people being mistakenly declared dead and carted off to the mortuary. The same thing can happen to a dream. You might run into an obstacle that appears insurmountable, but is it really? Could it be that your dream still has a pulse, but simply needs to be put on hold for a while (timing issues) or modified in some way (logistical issues)? It's always helpful to look around and see who, if anyone, has been able to overcome the challenge you're facing. You might be surprised.

But I also learned that if your dream really is dead, you need to face the truth.

Once a horse has died, there is no spur sharp enough to make it get up and run. This is what so many motivational speakers don't seem to get. They boil everything down to attitude and hard work, as if those two factors are all that's involved in dream chasing. Christians can be even more clueless at times, blaming a dream's death on the dreamer's lack of faith and condescendingly suggesting that the dream could be resuscitated if only the dreamer would channel more positive thoughts.

Let me just say right here that it's a terrible thing to dump a load of guilt onto someone who has just watched their dream die as a result of circumstances beyond their control. Almost always, that death will have been painful and bloody and emotional. The last thing the person needs is to be shamed and blamed for something he couldn't help.

And then, if you do come to the conclusion that your dream—as you dreamed it—is dead, allow yourself time to grieve.

As I look back on the death of my dream and its aftermath, I realize that I worked my way through the classic stages of grief, the same ones you would go through if a dear loved one passed away: denial, anger, bargaining, depression, and finally, acceptance. There will inevitably be some well-meaning friend in your life who will tell you to snap out of your funk and get on with your life, and you may feel that's exactly what you *want* to do. But the heart often lags behind the head. We often know what we *should* do long before we're able to marshal the resources to get it done. Don't rush this process. It has a way of unfolding in its own time.

And finally, when you're ready, start looking for a new dream.

I'll talk more about this later. For now, understand that the death of your dream doesn't mark the end of your life, only the end of your plans. And while you can't give yourself new life, you certainly

> The death of your dream doesn't mark the end of your life, only the end of your plans.

can make new plans. In my case, my dream died when I was still a teenager. According to the stats, I still had over five decades of life to fill! It would have been unthinkable to not start looking around for something else to do with my life.

As awful as my freshman recital was, when I went home with my family that night, there was a sense—though faint and feeble—that life would go on and that somehow, some way, someday, everything would be okay. Surely, my faith and the faith of my family was a part of this. My parents had long ago determined never to allow a victim mentality to take root in our home. Their prevailing sentiment is similar to that of Dietrich Bonhoeffer, the German pastor who opposed the rise of Nazism and was executed in prison by Heinrich Himmler at the age of thirty-nine. He said, "I believe that nothing that happens to me is meaningless, and that it is good for us all that it should be so, even if it runs counter to our own wishes."[3] Dad simply said it this way: "If something bad happens, suck it up and move on."

Still, the death of a dream is one of the hardest tests a person can face. Little did I know that the cave I found myself in was about to get deeper and darker.

making sense of **YOUR** *rhythm*

What do you do if your dream has died?

✦ Make sure your dream really is dead.

✦ If your dream really is dead, face the truth.

✦ Then you must allow yourself time to grieve.

Closing Encouragement

The death of your dream doesn't mark the end of your life, only the end of your plans. You can always make new plans.

We were even told, "Blessed are they that mourn," and I accepted it. I've got nothing that I hadn't bargained for. Of course, it is different when the thing happens to oneself, and in reality, not in imagination.[4]

—C. S. Lewis

three

the dead really do walk

Three months after the nightmare recital that marked the official burial of my dream, I was back on CSU's campus to drop off some household items I'd used in my dorm room the previous semester. Now that I was living at home, I didn't need the extra microwave, hamper, twin sheets, etc., so I decided to donate them to a campus group that distributed such items to new or needy students. There may have been a little generosity in that decision, but those items mainly brought back painful memories, and I just wanted to get rid of them.

I had planned to quickly drop the stuff off and leave, but the process took longer than I expected, causing me to be on campus after dark. When I finally walked out of the Lory Student Center to head for my car, I noticed that it was an unusually dark night. No moon, no stars, and more importantly, no working streetlamps along the walkway to my car. They were either malfunctioning or burned out.

As I moved from the ambient light of the student center into the deepening darkness, I had a sudden panic attack that was spurred by the realization that if an attacker sprung out of hiding and ran at me from behind, I wouldn't be able to hear him. I stopped and spun around, squinting into the darkness, almost certain that someone was there. I couldn't see anyone, but with quite a distance to go and an even darker stretch of sidewalk ahead, my courage failed and I beat a hasty retreat to the student center, where I stood under the one lamp that was burning and tried to calm myself.

This is silly, Mandy. It's a hundred and fifty feet to the car. No one is going to attack you. Just go. You need to get home.

But my feet were not buying it. They remained planted as securely as if my shoes had been encased in the concrete the day the cement was poured.

Again I stared into the darkness and didn't see a soul, but then an attacker would remain hidden until the last possible moment, wouldn't he? Perhaps he was crouching in the bushes, watching me at that very moment, willing me to move, whispering under his breath, *"Come on, my pretty . . . don't be afraid . . ."*

What happened next was straight out of a really bad horror movie.

I bolted.

I ran to the car as fast as I could, my heart slamming against the inside of my chest as hard as my feet were slamming

> Perhaps he was crouching in the bushes, watching me at that very moment, willing me to move, whispering under his breath, *"Come on, my pretty . . ."*

against the concrete. I skidded to a stop, fumbling for my keys, whipping my head from side to side, expecting to be pounced on by a deranged hybrid of Freddy Krueger and Michael Myers at any second. When I finally got into the car, I slammed the door and hit the locks, hyperventilating, shakily trying to get the keys into the ignition so I could get out of Dodge.

I tell you this story because it illustrates what I was experiencing as a fledgling member of the profoundly deaf community. I can sum it up in one word:

Loss.

It was as if my hearing had been the first domino to topple over and now the rest were falling in a terrifying chain reaction, one after another. Every day seemed to bring the realization of yet another treasured possession or ability that was gone forever.

In this instance, for example, it hit me like never before that I had lost the ability to hear what was going on behind me. That's not so important when you're in a familiar, safe, well-lit place. But when you're alone in the dark and you don't know who or what might be lurking nearby, you begin to realize that those two little satellite dishes mounted on the side of your head make up the most sophisticated early-warning system ever devised. To this day, I have a very real fear of someone creeping up behind me. If you notice me looking over my shoulder a lot, that's why.

Oh, but I'm just getting started. I also lost what I call the "soundtrack of everyday life."

I no longer hear the music they play in restaurants.

I don't hear birds singing or wind rustling the leaves.

I don't hear thunder booming in the sky or rain hitting the roof.

I don't hear the ominous rattle that tells me my car needs a mechanic.

I don't hear lawn mowers or car horns or planes passing overhead.

I don't hear the pulse-pounding music that adds suspense to a movie.

I don't hear the UPS guy ring my doorbell or the timer ding on the oven.

And in losing this audio ambiance, I've learned to appreciate how much we all depend on sound to get us through this life in one piece.

One day I was walking carefully down the middle of a sidewalk that had crusty ice and snow packed along its edges. Suddenly, I was flying through the air and then sprawling on the ground. I had no idea what hit me. It turned out that a bicyclist was pedaling toward me from behind, calling out, "On your left! On your left!" He assumed I heard him and would step to the right at the last moment. By the time he realized I wasn't hearing him, it was too late to avoid a collision. To his credit, I must say that he stopped and helped me up.

I also lost friends.

Part of the reason is that I became so hard to talk to. I had a tough time following conversations, and even when I was able to somewhat keep up by reading lips, I couldn't hear the inflection in people's voices. I couldn't tell if a comment was supposed to be serious or sarcastic. People would burst out laughing while I stood there clueless. The result is that people started directing their comments to everyone but me.

But mostly, I lost friends because they didn't know how to act around me. Should they talk louder or overexaggerate their mouth movements when speaking to me? Should they invite me if they were all going to a movie or a concert? Wouldn't such things be a waste of money for me? Wouldn't it just be a reminder of what I'd lost? And if I did decide to go, how would they talk to me in a dark theater or a dark car on the way home? I know all my friends wanted me to get better, but right or wrong, I couldn't help sensing that it was mostly because it would make *their* lives easier.

> Should they invite me if they were all going to a movie or a concert? Wouldn't it just be a reminder of what I'd lost?

I also lost the ability to sleep.

I would lie in bed and think about the fact that if someone tried to break into my home at 2:00 a.m., I wouldn't know it. If the fire alarm started screaming, I wouldn't know it. If a storm blew a tree limb through one of my windows in another part of the house, I wouldn't know it. If gunshots were fired on my front lawn, I wouldn't know it. Never before had my mind manufactured so many crisis scenarios, and most of them rolled off the assembly line when I laid down at the end of the day to close my eyes.

But the most important thing I lost was my identity.

For years, music had been my passion. It was on my mind all the time. No matter what I was doing, melodies and lyrics frolicked in my mind like kittens playing with a ball of yarn. Most of my friends were associated with music in some way. My heroes weren't athletes or movie stars, they were musicians. I have no doubt that if a scientist looked at my DNA, he would see little musical notes clinging to the strand because I was, from head to toe, a musician.

And then, suddenly, I wasn't.

Whereas before, everything in my life had somehow connected to music, all of a sudden nothing did. I was like an athlete who suffers a career-ending injury. One day he's taking snaps as an NFL quarterback and the next he's browsing through the want ads. He knows he's never again going to go to training camp or wear the uniform or hear the roar of the crowd. No longer can he call himself a ballplayer. At best, he is a *former* ballplayer, a relic, a has-been.

For me, this was devastating. I didn't know how to think about myself. I didn't know who I was staring at when I looked into a mirror. Even more frightening was the fact that I couldn't think of anything else I wanted to do. People would say, "Mandy, you're smart. You can do anything you want." I wanted to scream at them, "You mean I can do anything I *don't* want, because the only thing I *want* is to have a life in music!"

I eventually learned that music was not, in fact, my identity. It was my gift. I also came to understand that healthy, well-adjusted people can always reinvent themselves. They can find reasons for living outside of their gifts. But at the time I was neither healthy nor well adjusted. I was untethered, feeling like I had lost the only me I had ever known.

> I eventually learned that music was not, in fact, my identity. It was my gift.

The result of all this loss was a depression the likes of which I didn't even know existed. I had no appetite. I couldn't get out of bed. I didn't want to bathe. I didn't want to interact with people. I rarely went outside, causing my skin to become a clammy white color. People watch *The Walking Dead*, a show about zombies, and think they're watching fiction. I can assure you that the dead really do walk—at least from the bed to the bathroom to the couch. For me, those points pretty much marked the boundaries of my world.

One day I saw our family doctor, who noticed how sickly and pale I looked. He started asking questions, which ultimately led to him prescribing me an antidepressant. I understand his concern. Anyone could see I was lost. But the meds seemed like yet another blow because they made my hopelessness official. *Yes, Mandy, you really are one messed-up girl, and here are the drugs to prove it.*

At that point, six words haunted me: *You should be better than this.* I heard them in my head over and over again. Surely, someone who grew up in a minister's home with a solid foundation of faith and character should not be such a basket case. You hear stories all the time about heroes who conquer adversity like a hawk conquers a mouse. Why couldn't I be such a person?

Speaking of faith, I still went to church, of course. When your father is one of the ministers, there's no way you're staying home. But it was hard. I didn't pray, not because I was angry at God or had lost my faith, but because I simply had nothing to say to Him. I'd already said it all countless times. I figured saying it yet again would be pointless.

And then there were the people at church. Everyone was concerned about me, but they struggled to express it in a way that helped me. Some avoided me because they didn't know what to say, and others did what so many well-meaning people do: they spouted clichés. *"Just remember, honey, God never gives you more than you can han-*

dle!" I think I hated that one most of all. I felt like C. S. Lewis felt as he mourned the loss of his wife, Joy Davidman. He said, "Talk to me about the truth of religion and I'll listen gladly. Talk to me about the duty of religion and I'll listen submissively. But don't come talking to me about the consolations of religion or I shall suspect that you don't understand."

I also came to realize during this time that people didn't really want to know how I was doing. They would ask, but always in passing when they knew very well that there wasn't time to talk. I think one of the reasons they steered clear of any in-depth conversations was because my situation scared them. They didn't want to think about the fact that if something so terrible could happen to me, it could happen to them.

As I've said before, I don't blame them. It's hard to know what to say to someone who's going through a devastating life change. But for me, it was just another item on the list of things I had lost: meaningful interaction with friends.

This "walking dead" period of my life lasted about a year. The simplest way I can describe it is to say that all the color seemed to wash out of the world. Everything—and I do mean *everything*—seemed bland and uninteresting. Myself, most of all. But even this rock-bottom experience left me with two important things to say.

First, to anyone who might be going through a walking dead period: beware of radical responses to your situation.

It seems unthinkable, but there are beekeepers who don't put on all the protective gear that you would think would be necessary to keep from getting stung. Why? Because they know they can remain sting-free by keeping their movements very slow and deliberate. The main reason people get stung is because they spin around and wildly flail at the bees with their arms.

Likewise, in times of extreme duress, it's best not to flail. Too often, people respond to extreme pain with extreme actions. They run away, quit jobs, have affairs, abandon their values, and sometimes even commit suicide.

Let me encourage you not to do anything drastic during this dark period because there's a good chance the sun will shine again some-day. Things will get better, and you don't want to then have to pick up the pieces of a ruined life simply because you lost your composure in a moment of weakness. It's okay to feel sad, depressed, aimless, angry, or frustrated. But choices always matter, especially when there's al-ready trouble in your life. Don't com-pound it. A better approach is to try to find small victories in every day. They're there if you look for them.

> Let me encourage you not to do anything drastic during this dark period because there's a good chance the sun will shine again someday.

Second, I also want to speak to any-one who might love one of the walking dead: don't try to fix what's wrong.

So much of our culture revolves around fixing things. Think about the endless parade of "as seen on TV" products. From pillows that are designed to fix your insomnia to handheld kitchen gadgets that prom-ise a tear-free onion-chopping experience, we are bombarded with the notion that just about any problem has a quick and easy fix. And maybe some do. But when you find yourself living with one of the walking dead, you've got to recalibrate your thinking.

For one thing, realize that shortcutting a loved one's suffering (even if you could actually do it) would likely rob him or her of personal growth. Much of what I'm sharing in this book I learned over the long haul of my journey. If someone had stepped in and fixed everything for me early on, I would not be as emotionally and spiritually rich as I am today.

And never forget that your knowledge is limited. You might have an idea of what would fix your loved one's problem, but would it really? Or would it just make things worse? The words "I never intended for this to happen" are spoken all too frequently by people who meant well, but who likely plunged ahead with words and actions that were ill-advised.

The best thing you can do for a person who is stumbling through the darkness is to keep loving that person unconditionally and gently encourage her or him to keep making choices that will leave open the possibility of something good happening. This is what my parents did for me. They believed that things wouldn't always be so hard for me, that someday things would be better. But until that day came, they gently tried to keep me in a place where, if some wonderful opportunity or breakthrough did come along, I wouldn't miss it.

About a year into my life as a zombie something happened—in our basement, of all places—that changed everything.

making sense of **YOUR** *rhythm*

The dead really do walk . . .

- ✦ To those who feel they are the "walking dead"—don't respond to your extreme pain with extreme responses.

- ✦ To those who have a loved one who is the "walking dead"—don't try to fix what's wrong.

Closing Encouragement

Your passion is not your identity. It is your gift. When you get healthier, you can always reinvent yourself.

I have always been delighted at the prospect of a new day, a fresh try, one more start, with perhaps a bit of magic waiting somewhere behind the morning.

—J. B. Priestley

four

possibilities live
outside the box

People who have survived and overcome catastrophic experiences always have one thing in common: a turning point. They can tell you about a specific incident, sometimes even narrowing it down to the exact moment when their situation suddenly didn't look quite as hopeless. Mine happened in the basement of our family home.

My dad and I had set up an area for playing and recording music. It wasn't a studio, merely a quiet corner where we kept our guitars and a small TASCAM digital recorder. Before I lost my hearing, Dad and I would learn songs we liked and record them, him on guitar and me singing. Sometimes we would get fancy and overdub harmony vocals and a little fingerpicking. Just for fun, we would burn the songs onto CDs and give them to family members and friends for birthdays and Christmas. It wasn't a big deal. Never did we entertain the slightest notion of trying to do more than that with our recordings.

But when my ears decided to go out of business, this was another of life's sweet joys that I'd lost. Our little basement music-haven sat dark, our guitars in their cases, and we no longer had conversations about what songs we liked and might want to record.

What had been a cherished connection point with my dad was now gone, leaving a void that we didn't know how to fill. He was working long hours and trying to get his doctorate while I was drifting aimlessly, taking meds for depression, and slogging through some general education classes at Front Range Community College. Taking these college courses was not indicative of emotional or goal-setting progress on my part. I'd much rather have been lying in bed all day. But our family doesn't suffer victims gladly, and my mom hounded me to get up and do something whether I wanted to or not.

> What had been a cherished connection point with my dad was now gone, leaving a void that we didn't know how to fill.

Then, one day, out of the blue, Dad suggested that we go down to our little basement hideaway and make some music. I thought he was nuts. It was like asking a blind person to drive a car. But he was my dad, and I didn't want to just say no. I thought it would be better to give it a shot and fail. That way he could get the crazy notion out of his system and wouldn't keep bugging me about it.

To make things seem even more impossible, Dad encouraged me to pick a song I didn't know. That way I couldn't just rely on muscle memory, but would have to actually apply myself to the task of learning a song and truly think about how I might get over the obvious hurdles. I eventually chose a song that had become popular since I lost my hearing: "Come Home" by One Republic. It was a song my sister Sammi liked. I didn't know what it sounded like, but I figured it would do as good as any.

My big challenge was to figure out how, without my hearing, I could learn a new song and sing it on pitch in the right key. I didn't have much hope that I could. The whole idea seemed kind of silly, actually. But I did have an idea that I thought was worth trying. It involved sheet music and a guitar tuner.

The sheet music, which I had no trouble reading, showed me the melody and the time. The trick was finding the first note and then singing through the song, hitting all the correct intervals without drifting sharp or flat. For this I used the tuner. It would light up green when I was right on the note in question and red when I wasn't. I spent several hours singing the song over and over, checking myself with the tuner. After many tries, I was actually able to sing the correct notes—all the way through—and keep the light on the tuner green. I was pleased, of course, but it still didn't mean I would be able to sing with Dad's guitar accompaniment in a way that sounded good. So much of making music involves listening to the musicians around you and responding to little nuances.

Eventually, Dad and I sat down to see what we could do. I could tell he was excited, but I felt skeptical and uneasy. Yes, I was a bit curious after putting in so much time learning the song, but I was not optimistic.

Dad later shared with me how invested his heart was in this return to our little corner of the basement. And the reasons had nothing to do with music. He was heartbroken because he felt we had lost our connection, that my hearing loss had stolen the one thing we used to enjoy doing together. At the time, I didn't fully realize how he longed for us to take back some of that lost ground.

His heartbreak was also the reason—when we finally sat down to give the song a try—he decided to play my guitar, a Gibson SJ 100 acoustic that had been put away in its case for at least a year. That should have been my clue that, for Dad, this whole exercise was only a tiny bit about music. He could have used his own guitar, but he was obviously determined to drag into the light the things that had been swallowed up by the darkness, my guitar being one of them. Still, it was music we had come to play, and I had little hope that our efforts would amount to much.

The song "Come Home" is not difficult. Dad started playing the chords and I, with my guitar tuner in hand, started singing. I could see from the green light that I was on pitch, but being on pitch is not the same as sounding good. A foghorn can be on pitch, but no one wants to sit around and listen to it. Any musician knows that there's way more to making good music than just hitting the right notes. I couldn't tell if what we were doing had any "feel." I was watching Dad's hands for the rhythm and chord changes, but

I suspected the music was very stiff and mechanical, like an intermediate piano student who's hitting the right keys but without any nuance.

I suspected the music was very stiff and mechanical, like an intermediate piano student who's hitting the right keys but without any nuance.

I didn't know if what we'd accomplished was halfway decent or completely awful. The one thing I was sure of was that it wasn't great.

But Dad's reaction gave me pause. He didn't offer a high five or a knuckle bump. I had expected him to at least compliment my effort and offer words of encouragement. Instead, he sat there, frozen, with tears in his eyes.

And then he turned those eyes to me and said just four words: "Mandy, that was *beautiful*."

Things were never the same after Dad hit the STOP button on that recorder and gave me his first, honest impression of my performance. At that moment, a whole new world of possibilities opened up before us. No, we didn't sit there and talk about me having a singing career someday. But our little recording session did kick open a door that we thought had forever been nailed shut. At the very least, a dad and his daughter discovered that they could still make music, and at the very most . . . Well, that's just it—we didn't know at that moment what "very most" might happen, but we did believe that the door of possibilities had flung open, and we were confident that new adventures were somewhere out there, waiting to be discovered.

Challenging a deaf girl to learn a song she's never heard and to sing it with live accompaniment she can't hear is quintessential outside-the-box thinking. And that deaf girl accepting such a challenge turns it up a notch. Sometimes I think my dad and I did more than just climb out of the box; we wired it with explosives and pushed the plunger. It was that event that marked the turning point in my life, and it was at that moment that I began to believe that my possibilities definitely lived "outside the box."

Have you ever thought about your own box—the place or situation where you are most comfortable? I know all about the comfort of boxes. But boxes do just what their name says—they box us *in* and keep the world of possibilities *out*. Certainly, our boxes feel safe—and while comfortably in them, we avoid the risk of pain or failure. And not many people criticize us for hunkering down in our boxes, especially when we've suffered some kind of hardship or disability. They figure we've endured enough. If we choose to remain safely sequestered inside our boxes, who in his right mind would blame us?

But think, just imagine what possibilities live outside those boxes. And one of the amazing things about possibilities is that they love to morph and grow—if we just give them the room.

Just think how different your possibilities are now compared to when you started kindergarten. Sometimes our possibilities even morph and grow from one day to the next. Just ask a young attorney how different her possibilities looked the day after she passed the bar exam. Ask an amputee how different his possibilities looked the day after he was fitted with a prosthesis. From my journey, I've become aware of four reasons that possibilities *must* live outside the box.

The biggest reason is that there's just not enough room inside the box for expansion and growth.

Boundaries—limitations—are what make a box a box. And most of the inside-the-box people I've known fortify those boundaries with sentries and barbed wire. What chance do possibilities have to grow in a place like that?

Another reason possibilities must live outside the box is that they need room to run.

Possibilities are incurably frisky and love to lead you on a merry chase. Isn't that why we talk about people "chasing" their dreams? Thomas Edison, the Wright brothers, and even Walt Disney didn't experience success right out of the chute. They had to chase it down. They tried and failed and adapted and honed their efforts until they finally started showing some results.

In my case, the recording Dad and I made in our basement was only the first tiny baby step in a long journey that has led me to where I am today. And though I can't see what my future holds, it seems pretty obvious that the chase isn't over, that my possibilities are still in a running mood.

I've never met a truly committed inside-the-box person who was ever in a mood to give chase. Even if a possibility did go scampering by, the person who's in love with her box would more likely see that possibility as a threat than an opportunity. This is why relationships often become strained when people start pressuring their loved ones to climb out of the box. "Hurry up! There goes a possibility!" they shout. "You'll miss it if you don't get out of that box!" But their inside-the-box loved one recoils, saying, "Leave me alone! I'm happy the way I am!"

There's another thing we need to understand about possibilities. Besides *morphing and growing* and in addition to *running . . .*

Possibilities are free agents. And free agents can't find the best possibility partnership while in a box.

Every truly great accomplishment of humanity was at one time declared impossible. This means that more than one person encountered and passed on these possibilities, believing they were not worth the effort or, perhaps, were too far-fetched. No matter. Those free-agent possibilities simply move on, looking for someone with a broader mind and a bigger imagination.

> Those free-agent possibilities simply move on, looking for someone with a broader mind and a bigger imagination.

I've read that J. K. Rowling, the author of the Harry Potter books, was rejected by twelve different publishers before someone finally saw the possibilities in her work.

In 1962, the Beatles auditioned for Decca Records but were rejected. (Decca signed Brian Poole and the Tremeloes instead.)

Even a young Elvis Presley was told by the manager of the Grand Ole Opry that he would be better off returning to Memphis and driving a truck.

That's why possibilities have to be free to move around. Their value is unrecognized by many, and so they must keep knocking on doors until someone appreciates what they have to offer.

You will never, *ever* find possibilities living inside a box. So . . . if you want more out of life than you currently are getting, you must somehow find the courage to climb out of your box.

I use the word *courage* because that's what it really boils down to.

Do you have the courage to try something that might not work? Do you have the courage to risk adding a failure to your résumé? Do you have the courage to risk being embarrassed?

People who know the story of the basement recording Dad and I made have asked, "What if it hadn't worked?" Of course they're expecting us to say how devastated we would have been, which is why our answer surprises them. Dad and I both agree that nothing would have changed if that recording had not worked. We were already hurting. We were disconnected as father and daughter. I was on meds for depression. So what if our experiment flopped? Things couldn't have gotten much worse.

It's easier to do something daring when you don't have anything to lose.

Maybe it's time for you to try doing something different, something radical, something that will cause your friends to raise their eyebrows and call you crazy. Try it. Dare to throw your leg over the wall of that box you've set up house in and launch yourself out into a world where amazing things sometimes happen . . . where even girls who can't hear can have a singing career. I'll bet there's a possibility scampering by your box right now. What if you threw caution to the wind and took off after it?

G. K. Chesterton said, "There is one thing that gives radiance to everything. It is the idea of something around the corner."[5] But there will never be anything around the corner until we get out from between the four corners that are hemming us in.

making sense of YOUR *rhythm*

Why possibilities only live "outside the box":

+ There's not enough room for growth inside the box.

+ Possibilities need room to run.

+ Possibilities are free agents, in search of someone with a broad mind and a big imagination.

Closing Encouragement

There is one thing that gives radiance to everything. It is the idea of something around the corner.[6]

—G. K. Chesterton

*Say **Yes** and you'll figure it out afterwards.*[7]

—Tina Fey

you can only become
what you're willing to try

There are two schools of thought when it comes to the potency of words. One says that words are so powerful they can change the course of history. Hence every author's favorite rallying cry, "The pen is mightier than the sword!" The other is that even the most hateful words are no more fearsome than a kitten. Hence the adage that has been shouted on elementary school playgrounds since Cain and Abel were fifth graders: "Sticks and stones may break my bones, but words can never hurt me!"

So who's right?

I suppose it depends on one's experience. Mine tells me that words are extraordinarily powerful, especially one little three-letter beauty that has changed my life. I'm talking about the word *yes*.

Not that I don't have a lot of respect for the word *no*. Goodness, we could do with a few more nos in this world, couldn't we? Every time I hear that some politician or pastor has been caught in a scandal, or some other easily avoidable tragedy takes over the news cycle, I remember the power of *no*.

But *yes* is my favorite word because it is the force that propelled me from my life of disillusionment into the wonderful, interesting life I enjoy today.

It started with that little recording Dad and I made in the basement.

That was my first *yes*.

But when he said it was *beautiful*, I had my doubts. I mean, I kind of believed he meant it because I know him to be a man of truth and integrity. But I also know how much he loves me. I knew his heart might overrule his head and compel him to take a rosier view of our little song than was warranted. So I decided to do what most people do in that situation . . . get a second opinion.

I decided to take the recording to Cynthia Vaughn, a private voice teacher in Fort Collins, from whom I had taken lessons when I was in high school. She'd been heartbroken by my hearing loss because she knew, better than most people, how much I loved music and singing. She was and is a good friend, and I trusted her opinion. I knew she'd give it to me straight. And besides, I hadn't seen her in a while and wanted to let her know I was going to be okay.

I'd heard that she was opening a new music studio, so I dropped in on the day of the grand opening to help her celebrate her new venture. I thought that if I got there early, she might find three minutes to listen to the song. Not surprisingly, she was hustling and bustling, trying to take care of several last-minute details. She told me to play the

song and that she would listen while she worked. It wasn't the scenario I was hoping for, but what could I do?

When the song finished playing, she said, "That was nice. You recorded it before you lost your hearing." It was a statement, not a question.

"No," I said. "We recorded it last week."

Cynthia stopped what she was doing. "Last week? Are you serious?"

"Yes."

"Play it again."

This time Cynthia stopped what she was doing and listened atten-
tively. I could tell from the look on her face that she was impressed,
so much so that she was full of questions. Unfortunately, her grand
opening was about to begin, so we put our conversation on hold until
it was over. I hadn't intended to stay through the whole thing, but
I did, and when it ended we talked. The big thing that came out of
our conversation was Cynthia's suggestion that I start taking voice lessons again. She said I obviously still had some ability and the lessons
might help me figure out what I was capable of and what direction
I might want to go with my singing.

I wasn't sure I wanted to do it. Making recordings in the basement with Dad was one thing, but was there really any reason to think
I might be able to do more? I didn't want to waste my time, or Cynthia's, but she was insistent, so mostly just to please her, I agreed.

That was my second *yes*.

At this point I should tell you that Cynthia's forte is classical and
show music. She's an extraordinary performer and teacher, but I had

developed an interest in jazz before I lost my hearing, and if I was going to try to sing, that was the direction I wanted to go. At my second lesson, I sang "My Funny Valentine," one of my favorite songs. Cynthia was impressed enough that she came up with what I thought was a perfectly absurd idea: that I should go to a place in Fort Collins called Jay's Bistro and sing a song on open mike night.

> She came up with a perfectly absurd idea . . . I should go to Jay's Bistro and sing a song on open mike night.

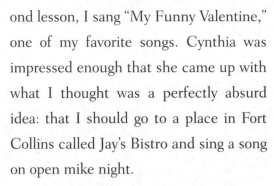

Jay's Bistro is a restaurant and jazz lounge that features live music. The house pianist was Mark Sloniker, an unbelievable musician, one of those people who has a seemingly effortless talent. He can play anything and make it look easy. What business I had sharing a stage with someone like him was beyond my comprehension. Still, Cynthia thought I should give it a shot. She assured me that with Mark's talent I would be in good hands. He'd be able to follow me and bail me out if I got completely lost. It was silly, I thought. No one in her right mind would make the leap from an amateur basement recording to singing in front of a live audience who is accustomed to listening to real, accomplished musicians. But I thought again about that *box*, and I agreed to do it—partly so I wouldn't disappoint Cynthia and partly because she assured me that on open mike night there would be only a half-dozen people there who would be distracted by their eating and drinking while I sang.

That was my third *yes*.

I was so nervous that I threw up before it was my turn to sing at

Jay's. This is often how my body reacts to panic. I've thrown up more times than I care to count. I cleaned myself up and asked myself what I was doing there. How did I let Cynthia talk me into this? Maybe I could just get up and walk out. Surely no one would blame me for changing my mind. But before I could turn around, I saw Mark Sloniker beckoning me toward the stage with his index finger.

Mark was a sweetheart. Nothing was said to the audience about my deafness, but he knew my situation, so he helped me find my starting note. I always start with middle C, a note I can usually find in my head, and go up or down the scale from there. He nodded when I hummed a B-flat, the starting note, and then went into what I know must have been a beautiful introduction to "My Funny Valentine." I stood right next to the piano, holding on to it so I could feel the vibrations, and I patted my foot to stay in tempo. And I was shaking. Boy, was I shaking! It's a good thing I had already thrown up because if I'd had anything left in my stomach, those patrons would have likely had more than music to talk about on their way home.

At the end of the evening, Jay, the owner, and Mark told me I'd done great and needed to come back, next time singing more than one song. I felt encouraged by this because I couldn't think of any reason either of them would want to humor me. They'd been doing their thing for years. They didn't need me and had no reason to lug me along if they felt I was deadweight. Based on that logic, I agreed to try it again, this time with a couple of different songs.

That was my fourth *yes*.

My next open mike night went so well that I was invited to sing at the club every week. It seemed like a wonderful opportunity, but the club was an hour and a half from where I lived, and I was working a full-time job. I would also have to continually work up new material because many of the patrons at Jay's were regulars, and I knew they would complain if I sang the same songs over and over. So saying yes to that opportunity would put tremendous pressure on me. I would be taking on a ton of extra work. I wasn't sure if I was up to it, but after giving it a lot of thought, I eventually agreed.

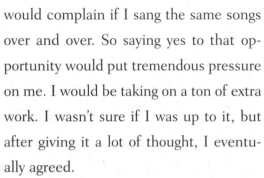

> I wasn't sure if I was up to it, but after giving it a lot of thought, I eventually agreed. That was my fifth *yes*.

That was my fifth *yes*.

Once I started singing regularly at the club, I began to develop a small following: patrons who liked my singing and would always be there anytime I was on the schedule. One sweet old guy named Gerry bounced from one music venue to another all around the area, but he was always at Jay's when I performed and always requested "Bye Bye Blackbird."

With my little following starting to grow, I was invited to start doing full, three-hour concerts. This, as you can imagine, gave me pause. Three hours' worth of material is a lot of songs, which means a lot of work. And three hours' worth of singing would challenge vocal cords that were made out of piano wire. Still, it was an honor to be asked, and I was enjoying the whole Jay's experience, so I agreed.

That was my sixth *yes*.

Then came the suggestion that I make a CD.

At this point we were venturing into territory that seemed light-years away from the little basement hideaway where Dad and I made our recording of "Come Home." Who would have thought that so many opportunities would come my way? Especially since I never really wanted to be a performer. I always wanted to be a music teacher, a choir director. Not once when I was young did I see myself as the lounge singer I had suddenly become. And now a CD? It sounded so exciting, but that excitement was tempered by the fact that it was going to cost me thousands of dollars to do it right, with the best musicians and first-class packaging. Still, I agreed to do the CD and titled it *Smile*.

That was my seventh *yes*.

That CD must have turned out pretty well because it wasn't long before people started asking for another.

Each one of these opportunities required a deliberate decision to say *yes*. It wasn't easy to say yes. I was scared. I was full of doubts. I wasn't sure why the opportunities were coming my way. I certainly wasn't sure I had the ability to do all the things I was being invited to do. In each and every case, I could think of multiple reasons to say no. Sometimes I thought I probably needed to have my head examined. Yet in each instance, something deep inside me compelled me to say yes, and all of those yeses piled one on top of the other and eventually led me to an amazing place.

If you feel that your life is going nowhere, maybe it's because you've been saying no when you need to be saying yes. It could be because you doubt yourself or because the opportunities coming your way don't fit with the plan you had laid out for your life. (Believe me, I can relate!) Or maybe it's simply because your nature is to play it safe, to avoid risks. Maybe you've said yes a time or two in the past and gotten burned. Whatever your reasons for saying no, I want to encourage you to start throwing some yeses into the mix.

Now, I'm not suggesting that you be reckless or foolish. In fact, I'd like to share a few guidelines—lessons I learned from the events related earlier—that will help you know when to say yes.

First, my yeses were to opportunities that made sense sequentially.

In other words, I didn't go from making an amateur recording in our basement to making a CD in one step. There were lots of smaller steps along the way. Likewise, when an opportunity comes your way, you should be able to see that it makes some kind of sequential sense. Ask yourself if it's the logical next step. Almost everything important that's accomplished in this world is done one step at a time.

> Almost everything important that's accomplished in this world is done one step at a time.

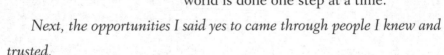

Next, the opportunities I said yes to came through people I knew and trusted.

In some cases, the only reason I said yes was because I didn't want to let someone I loved down, as in the case of my dad asking me to try singing again in the basement. When an opportunity comes your way, thoughtfully assess the person making the offer. Is it someone you know? Someone you trust? Someone you like? Someone who has a proven track record? Or is it someone your friends are warning you about? Someone who stands to make a lot of money off your efforts? Someone who seems to have swooped in out of nowhere just when your potential started to show itself? Only say yes when you feel comfortable with the person making the offer.

Finally, all of the opportunities I said yes to fit somewhat with my abilities and dreams.

I say they were "somewhat" fitting because these opportunities did stretch me. I found myself doing things I never thought I'd ever do. But it was all still about music, that thing I loved so much and that had driven so many of my hopes and dreams since childhood.

So when I encourage you to start saying yes more often, I'm not suggesting that you be foolish or reckless. You can live your life aggressively and chase after opportunities without abandoning common sense.

More than anything, saying yes is about overcoming your fears and believing in yourself. If people whom you know and trust think enough of your ability to give you a chance, and if that opportunity speaks to your heart and feeds into your dreams, go for it!

I want to share one significant detail about all my trips from my home in Longmont to Fort Collins to sing at Jay's Bistro. As I said, it's about an hour-and-a-half drive, depending on traffic, and it took me right past the campus of Colorado State University, that place where I had suffered so much trauma, where I had lost my hearing and my dream and my identity. To be honest, I found it very painful to drive by the campus. I had flashbacks at first. I even made it a point to circumvent the campus for a while so I wouldn't have to look at the very buildings where my world went horribly wrong.

Now, looking back, I have a much greater appreciation for that little touch of geographical irony, the graveyard of my old life and the launching pad of my new life sitting so close together. I believe driving past the campus every time I went to Jay's engraved an important truth in my mind. Namely, that even though life has the power to say no, it can't stop me from continuing to say yes. And if I say enough yeses, they will eventually outweigh life's nos.

making sense of **YOUR** *rhythm*

Figuring out when it's wise to say YES:

+ Make sure you're saying yes to the next logical, sequential step.

+ Only say yes to opportunities that come through people you know and trust.

+ It's okay that the opportunity stretches you, but make sure it *somewhat* fits your abilities and dreams.

Closing Encouragement

Even though life has the power to say no, it can't stop you from continuing to say yes. And if you say enough yeses, they will eventually outweigh life's nos.

The Bible tells us to love our neighbors, and also our enemies; probably because they are generally the same people.[8]

—G. K. Chesterton

six

dream thieves lurk
in unexpected places

My first CD, *Smile*, was a major accomplishment for me. People can judge for themselves how good or bad it is, but no one can diminish the accomplishment. From losing my hearing and thinking I would never have anything more to do with music for the rest of my life to recording a jazz CD with world-class musicians was a long, hard, often painful climb. Most people who know me will tell you I'm not an egotistical person, yet I will admit I was proud of that CD and did what anyone would do in that situation: I posted it on Facebook.

Naturally, my close friends and family members rejoiced with me. What surprised me was the negativity that came hurtling at me from out of the anonymity of cyberspace. One email in particular was especially troubling. It accused me of doing one of three things. Either I was running from my identity as a deaf person (which the email sender considered an insult to all deaf people), or I was using my hearing loss for personal gain, or I was just pretending to be deaf so I could gain an advantage in my career with a sad story. The email concluded by saying that doing any one of those three things made me a despicable person who did not deserve to be sucking up the world's oxygen. It wasn't exactly a death threat, but it wasn't a far miss.

Then one night at the end of one of my sets at Jay's Bistro, I walked outside to get a little air. I saw a group of people about my age on the sidewalk, signing. I thought I recognized one of them from my American Sign Language classes, so I walked over to say hi. She greeted me and asked what I was doing. When I told her I'd just finished singing at Jay's, her eyes popped open in surprise.

"I thought you were deaf," she said.

"I am."

"Then why are you singing? Why are you chasing music?"

I knew what she was really asking. Her question was based on the premise that, as a deaf person, I should fully embrace the deaf culture and celebrate my deafness rather than trying to escape it by making a name for myself in the hearing world. She interpreted my singing at Jay's as an attempt to fix what was broken in my life. And if there's one thing some deaf people hate, it's the implication that they are somehow broken.

I can honestly say she was wrong in her assessment of me. I was singing for one reason and one reason only: music is embedded in my soul and is constantly scratching and clawing, trying to get out. That's it, pure and simple. Philosophical assessments of the deaf community and my role in it were a million miles from my mind. And I wasn't trying to imply through my singing that deaf people were in any way broken. I just wanted to make music.

The conversation ended with her stomping off. I admit that I was really shaken. This young woman clearly thought I was a disgusting excuse for a deaf human being. That kind of experi-

I wasn't trying to imply through my singing that deaf people were in any way broken. I just wanted to make music.

ence is a punch in the gut for anyone. But when—like me—you want to be liked, it's devastating.

I share these stories because they illustrate a simple truth that I have become very aware of since I lost my hearing: dream thieves lurk in unexpected places.

That dream thieves exist is no surprise, of course. The world is full of jealous, small-minded people who don't like seeing anyone but themselves succeed. But when they pop up in places where you'd normally expect to find love and support, their existence can be a real shock. The pain and discouragement often derails the tentative dreamer.

We all know people who've had dream thieves for parents. "You're no good; you'll never amount to anything," they say as they berate their children.

Or how about the so-called friend who's never had a dream of her own and thinks, therefore, that you're being reckless? "You need to get this dream foolishness out of your head and settle down and be like me. You're going to get hurt," she warns.

And then there's the boyfriend who feels threatened by your

dream. "If you chase your dream, then what happens to mine?" he whines.

Parents and friends and romantic partners aren't supposed to rain on your parade. They aren't supposed to stand on the ground firing at your helium-filled balloons with a BB gun as you're floating off toward your dream. They're supposed to support you, and even if they don't understand your dream or agree with it, you want them to allow you to discover for yourself if it's a good one or a bad one.

The pages of history are filled with stories of people who accomplished great things even as those around them warned them that what they were trying to do would never work. How many people ridiculed Christopher Columbus and warned him that he would sail off the edge of the earth? How many people laughed at the Wright brothers and their silly contraptions? How many people scoffed at the notion that a theme park based on a cartoon mouse would be successful?

So what's the best way to respond to dream thieves, especially those you assumed would be on your side? I think I've learned a few things about this.

First, people's criticism is often more a reflection of their own heart than it is your actions.

Take the young woman who chastised me on the sidewalk outside of Jay's Bistro. I get where she was coming from. There is a segment of the deaf community that draws a distinction between *Deafness* and *deafness* (capital *D* versus lowercase *d*). *Deafness*, with a capital *D*, refers to people who have been deaf from either birth or the age of two or under. They have either one or two deaf parents.

Lowercase *deafness* refers to people like me, who were not born deaf and who do not have deaf parents. What this creates is a feeling in some Deaf people that a person like me is not deaf enough. They see my singing career as a rejection of the Deaf community and an attempt to be accepted by the hearing community. They also see my singing as an exploitation of my deafness for personal gain, which they find highly offensive.

Some Deaf people think that a person like me is not deaf enough.

People are free to believe whatever they want. What's unfortunate is when their point of view becomes a reason to try to hold other people back.

I've read that lobsters can be kept in containers that do not have a lid because they refuse to let each other escape. Whenever one starts to crawl out, another will grab him and pull him back in. I cannot explain the science behind this, but I know it's not unique to lobsters. People do it, too, and when it happens, it says more about the one doing the pulling than the one being pulled.

Next, I've learned that a small minority of people can have a devastating impact on your life—but only if you let them.

We might tend to think that the word *minority* is synonymous with weakness, but nothing could be further from the truth. In fact, the term "dominant minority" is used by sociologists to describe the often amazing power that people can have even though they are greatly outnumbered. One good example would be the Nazi Party in Germany in the 1930s. The vast majority of Germans were not Nazis and wanted nothing to do with war, but they were dragged into the war anyway. Another example would be the white South Africans, who, before 1994, controlled South Africa even though they never comprised more than 22 percent of the population. Just because people are outnumbered does not mean that they do not have power.

It's likely that you will never have a large group of dream thieves in your life. In truth, most people won't care what you do. They have too many of their own worries to spend time thinking about you. But the small number of dream thieves you do encounter could become the dominant minority if you let them.

I've also learned that it's wise to listen to and evaluate all criticism.

Even the Deaf culture that has a problem with me because of my singing has a point of view, and even though I disagree with it, I am a better person for taking the time to think it through and understand it. The key is to filter all the criticism you receive through the sifter of your own values and not allow a vocal minority to have a disproportionate amount of influence on your life.

Then there's this: real friends never threaten you with expulsion simply because you disagree with them and choose your own path.

So . . . there may be some times that we have to risk alienating certain people. That word *alienate* is a strong one. It communicates more than just a mild disagreement. More often than not, it signals the death of the relationship. That's a heavy thing to contemplate, especially if you're talking about someone you've previously loved or respected. Some people are so unsettled by the thought of losing a friend that they acquiesce to the dream thief's wish just to keep the relationship alive.

But there's a question that needs to be asked: If a person would write you off as a friend simply because you had the courage to think for yourself and make your own choice, does she (or he) even qualify as a friend? In what universe do friends demand total agreement from each other? In what universe does one friend condemn another for reaching for the stars? In my opinion, any person who would threaten me with alienation if I go ahead and chase my dream is not a friend at all.

Any person who would threaten me with alienation if I go ahead and chase my dream is not a friend at all.

It seems to me that we should elevate our thinking with regard to friendship. A person is not my friend simply because Facebook says she is or because she follows me on Twitter or Instagram. A person is not my friend simply because we've gone to school together or worked in the same office or attended the same church. And a person is certainly not my friend simply because we share a disability. My real friends know my heart. They see my imperfections and love me anyway. And while they always feel free to tell me what they think, they never threaten me with expulsion from their lives if I disagree and choose my own path.

Here's one final thought on dream thieves—and then let us be done with them! In addition to not allowing people to steal your dreams . . .

Don't allow others to scare you into shrinking your dreams.

In 1957, a science fiction movie was released called *The Incredible Shrinking Man*. Based on a book by Richard Matheson, it tells the story of an ordinary man who suddenly realizes he's getting smaller and smaller. Eventually, he's so small that his own house cat becomes the equivalent of a terrifying monster.

Obviously, people don't shrink, at least not in the way that movie suggests. But dreams sometimes do. I've known people who started out with a big dream, but by the time their friends and acquaintances got through pointing out all the problems they were likely to face, they decided to scale it way back.

I wonder how many times the following arguments have been made:

"You say you want to be a doctor, but do you realize how much money it will cost and how many years it will take? You'll be paying off your school debt until you're in your fifties! Don't you think you'd be better off becoming a pharmacist?"

"I know it's a great job they're offering you, but you'd never be happy living in the city. It's not safe. And just think how much higher the cost of living would be. Wouldn't it be better to make less money and live in a smaller, safer town?"

"Are you sure you want to own your own business? Remember, if you're the owner, all the problems land in your lap and all the bills land on your desk. You could still do the work you enjoy if you worked for someone else."

It's okay if you modify your dream because your heart is telling you to. Sometimes that happens when you get sound advice from someone you trust. But it's not okay to modify your dream because some dream thief is trying to scare you.

Most people who point out all the problems you're likely to face as you chase your dream have not actually chased your particular dream themselves. The person who talks about how awful it would be to live in the city may have never actually lived in one. The person who talks about the headaches involved in owning a business may never have owned one. They're speaking from their impressions rather than their experiences, yet they want you to take their word as gospel.

Whatever you have in mind to do with your life, understand that the first person you have to reckon with is yourself:

What are you doing that might keep you from getting where you want to go?

What bad habits are keeping you from being your best?

What details are you not paying attention to?

What wise advice are you not listening to?

What disciplines are you neglecting?

It does no good to identify other people who might be dream thieves if the biggest thief of all stares back at you every time you look in the mirror.

Experience tells me that the world favors people who have big dreams and refuse to let others tamper with them. If you have a dream right now, guard it with your life. Don't let anyone—even someone who loves you—steal it. And don't let someone convince you to whittle it down to a size *they* feel comfortable with.

It's *your* dream, not theirs.

making sense of
YOUR *rhythm*

Remember these truths with dealing with dream thieves:

+ People's criticisms are often more a reflection of their own heart than of your actions.

+ Dream thieves are a small minority and can only deter you if you let them.

+ It's wise to listen to and evaluate all criticism, but filter it through the sifter of your own values.

+ Real friends never threaten you with expulsion simply because you disagree with them and choose your own path.

+ Don't allow others to scare you into shrinking your dream down to *their* size.

Closing Encouragement

The world favors people who have big dreams and refuse to let others tamper with them. If you have a dream right now, guard it with your life.

Better to put your heart on the line, risk everything, and walk away with nothing than play it safe. Love is a lot of things, but "safe" isn't one of them.[9]

—Mandy Hale

seven

playing it safe is the greatest risk of all

*T*his is the chapter I've been dreading.

I knew when I agreed to write this book that I would have to make some hard choices along the way, to share or not to share certain painful experiences from my life. Some people believe that sharing a painful experience with the world somehow cleanses it out of your system. Maybe it works that way sometimes, but I suspect it's just as often true that allowing the world in on your most painful secrets makes the pain even worse. If nothing else, the remembering takes you back to a time you want nothing more to do with and allows the person who hurt you one more opportunity to bring you pain.

I decided that I would make my choices on these matters based on whether or not I felt the experience offered a meaningful lesson that might help someone. What you're about to read now is not the proudest chapter of my life, but I'm confident it will speak powerfully to a lot of people who are contemplating major, life-altering decisions. Specifically, I want to tell you about my first marriage. I was just twenty-two years old and, as failures go, this one was epic.

But first, one ground rule: I've decided I'm not going to use my ex's name.

And I've decided to handle this the way my family handled it.

If you're a fan of the Harry Potter books, you know that Voldemort is Harry's central antagonist, his archenemy. The witches and wizards won't even utter his name. They call him "You-Know-Who" or "He-Who-Must-Not-Be-Named." In my family, this is the name we have given my ex. We didn't do it out of malice, but in an attempt to bring a little levity into what is an otherwise painful memory. And besides, I wouldn't be surprised if You-Know-Who has a few names for me. No marital catastrophe is all one person's fault, right? So, I must sheepishly admit that I made my share of mistakes, too.

Let me start near the end of our story, with one of the most painful experiences of my life.

I'd been at the studio and was returning home with the final mix of my second CD. It still had to be mass-produced, but at least we finally had the music the way we wanted it. This is an exciting time for any musician. You put in so much time and effort, knocking yourself out to make sure everything is perfect, and then, finally, after countless playbacks and tweaks, you know you've nailed it. Plus, I was especially excited about that CD because some of the songs I chose had special meaning for me. I couldn't wait to get home and let You-Know-Who hear it.

I walked into our apartment at 10:00 p.m.

The first thing I noticed was that one of our two dogs was gone.

Then I noticed that You-Know-Who's laptop was missing.

And his books.

I felt a spike of apprehension in my chest as I tore through the apartment, confirming what I somehow sensed I would find: that all of his stuff had been moved out.

At that point, I began looking for a note. There was no way he would move out and not leave a note, even if it was just to tell me what a loser of a wife I was. But apparently he did. I searched high and low, but couldn't find a note anywhere.

I found myself standing there in our apartment, minus a dog, minus a husband, minus a note, and minus every bit of the excitement I'd been feeling only seconds earlier. I had no idea where my husband had gone, or whether he was even okay. Did he run off with another woman? Did he kill himself? I had no idea. This was not something I'd been anticipating.

Then I looked down at the CD I still held in my hand and noticed the title scrawled on the shiny disc: *After You've Gone*.

I looked down at the CD I still held in my hand and noticed the title scrawled on the shiny disc: *After You've Gone*.

Sometimes life's ironies are just too much.

Naturally, I took to my phone and started trying to locate You-Know-Who. I called and texted, but there was no answer. So I called and texted again and then again. Finally, I guess I managed to annoy him enough that he texted back and said he was okay, that he just needed some time. He asked for one week to think things through.

That day ended with me sitting in the bathtub alongside Annie, my service dog. I was crying, and she was surely wondering why I was so upset.

If you've ever experienced a moment like that (and I hope you haven't), you know that the flashbacks begin immediately. You start remembering and reliving moments from your time together—even going back to the very beginning of your relationship—trying to figure out what went wrong. Were there signs I missed? Was he not who I thought he was? Was the whole thing *my* fault? Had I been such a terrible wife that I couldn't keep a man happy long enough to even celebrate our first anniversary?

I had known that our marriage wasn't fairy-tale material. Both of us were dealing with frustrations. But silly me, I thought that was normal for newlyweds. I'd heard my whole life that the first year of marriage is the hardest and you have to be prepared to make a lot of adjustments. And I certainly didn't think our marriage would be any different. But apparently it was. We didn't even make it to the six-month mark. Even the most catastrophic relationships often last at least a year, don't they?

Let me take you back to the beginning.

It all started when I went to a Deaf social in Superior, Colorado. The purpose of a Deaf social is to provide an environment that nurtures the strong sense of Deaf identity that members of the Deaf community have. All communication at a Deaf social is through signing or writing, relieving the Deaf person from the pressure of having to lip-read. I was required to go to the social as an assignment for an American Sign Language class I was taking, but I really enjoyed it. It was at this social that I met You-Know-Who.

He introduced himself to me, and I soon learned that he was a leader in the Deaf community. He organized Deaf socials, including the very one we were attending. Quickly, we became friends. There was no romantic aspect to our relationship. It was simply that we had a lot in common and moved in the same circles. One year went by, and then two. During that time, You-Know-Who was a mentor to me, very protective and sweet, almost like I was his little sister.

I liked him for a few reasons. One, he wasn't a complicated person. He wasn't a bundle of contradictions like some people I've known. His opinions were pretty consistent. He didn't require a lot of analysis. He was a pretty easy guy to understand. The last thing I needed in my already challenging life was a friend with a personality like a Rubik's Cube. If he had been that, I would have run for the hills.

He also seemed to respect me as a woman, which was no small thing. Never did he try to leverage our friendship to get sex, for example. He seemed content with just being friends, which I appreciated.

He wasn't a believer in Jesus, and was in fact dismissive of religion in general. But the friendship we shared, the interest he took in me, the respect he showed me, and the things I learned from him seemed to counterbalance my concerns about his antagonism toward my faith. And besides, we were just friends. It wasn't like we were going to get married or anything.

Until, suddenly, we were.

It happened near the end of our second year as friends. We were riding in the car together when You-Know-Who mentioned that we ought to get married. There was no romantic proposal, no carefully prepared, heart-tugging speech. He didn't so much "pop" the question as just casually throw it out there. If he'd said, "Let's go to the movies," he'd likely have done it with the same amount of intensity. Instantly, I had a lot to think about.

And this is where we get to the crux of the matter.

As long as we were just friends, I had no trouble ignoring his less attractive qualities. They didn't affect me much because I wasn't his wife or mother, so I could overlook them and enjoy the more positive aspects of our friendship. And I could leave if he got on my nerves too much. But the instant he proposed marriage, I was forced to factor in how I would like being married to a guy who had some glaring weaknesses.

For example, during the time we were friends, he didn't work. I did. I worked myself half to death on some very menial jobs, but he didn't. That's why, when we decided to get married, I had to buy my own engagement ring. What girl does that? It embarrasses me to admit that I did, but it's true. My only defense is that if we'd announced our engagement without a ring, everyone would have asked about it, requiring an embarrassing explanation. And I knew if we waited until he could afford to pay for it, we might be celebrating our second or third wedding anniversary. It was just easier to buy the crazy thing myself.

I could go on with other examples, but I don't want to dwell on his weaknesses because I have my own and, besides, his weaknesses aren't the point—*my judgment is*. In spite of there being more red flags flapping in my face than you'd find at the United Nations, I chose to marry You-Know-Who. The wedding happened about a year after he proposed. There were close to six hundred people in attendance.

Our marriage was never really good, at least not the kind of good you dream of when you're a little girl. Employment always seemed to elude him. He didn't like me spending time with my family. He didn't help around the house. He barely fed or walked the dogs. He made decisions and spent money without consulting me. He ran around with his own friends but protested if I wanted to hang out with mine. Even so, I naively believed everything would be fine after we figured each other out and made some adjustments.

And then he left.

If there's one thing I know, it's that a failed marriage will turn you into a philosopher. I couldn't begin to count the hours that I sat around and pondered what went wrong. Socrates and Plato would have been proud. Eventually, I found my way to what I believe to be the cold, hard truth: the biggest mistake I made was that I played it safe.

> I found my way to the cold, hard truth: the biggest mistake I made was that I played it safe.

You-Know-Who was, to me, a safe choice for a boyfriend and a husband.

One reason is because he apparently *wanted* to be my boyfriend and husband, and no one else had ever shown any interest. I hear women talk about their high school and college days when they were dating guys and going to parties. I never did any of that. Even when I met You-Know-Who, I'd never been asked out on a date before. So yes, even though he had some drawbacks, I was interested because I thought that if I let this one get away, there might never be another. Maybe you have to be a single woman to understand what a powerful factor that is.

A second reason—the biggest reason—why I felt You-Know-Who was a safe choice is because he, too, was deaf. I knew he would understand the life I live, that I wouldn't always have to be explaining my feelings and frustrations to him the way I might if I married a man who could hear. Unless you have a disability, you might not realize what a big thing this is. There's very little understanding in this world as it is, but even less if you have a disability. It seemed heavenly to think that I might be able to live my life with a man who totally "got" me.

So, as crazy as it sounds when I describe his faults, he still seemed like a safe choice. I understand now that playing it safe is the biggest risk of all. Here are three hard-earned observations that will help you understand why.

First, safe *is often just a code word for* easy.

The "safe" route is often just the one that requires less time and effort. This was certainly the case for me. By pairing up with You-Know-Who, I wouldn't have to wait for anyone else or look for anyone else. I wouldn't have to sit around and wonder if there would ever *be* anyone else. I wouldn't have to suffer the pain of always being the single girl in a group of couples. I wouldn't have to endure a constant parade of friends offering to fix me up with some friend of a friend.

You will do much better in life if you always remember that *safe* often means *easy* and that *easy* rarely gets you where you want to go. Name anything worthwhile, and I doubt you'll find the word *easy* attached to it.

Getting a college degree? Not easy.

Building a thriving business? Not easy.

Raising great kids? Not easy.

Finding your soul mate and building a great marriage? Definitely not easy.

The second thing I learned is that playing it safe eliminates the possibility that life could surprise you.

Have you seen the game show where they offer the contestant her choice of prizes? She can take the coffee maker or choose what's hidden behind the curtain. The safe choice is the coffee maker, of course. If you choose it, you know you're not going to go home empty-handed. But you might also be missing out on a brand-new car or a Hawaiian vacation.

This is pretty much how life works. There's what's right in front of you, and then there's what you can't see . . . what's out there just over the horizon. If you always play it safe and grab what's right in front of you, you accumulate a lot of coffee makers, but you eliminate the possibility of ever winning the big prize.

> There's what's right in front of you, and then there's what you can't see . . . what's out there just over the horizon.

Third, I learned that what appears to be safe might actually be the most dangerous thing of all: "safe" is not always easy to identify.

For example, would you rather go skydiving or go racing down the interstate at seventy miles an hour surrounded by distracted drivers who are speeding, messing with their phones, and weaving in and out of traffic? I'd be willing to bet that most people would choose the highway, thinking that skydiving is just too dangerous, even though about four hundred thousand people die in car accidents every year compared to about twenty who die while skydiving. When you skydive, there are one or two things that can go wrong. When you're flying down the interstate, there are a thousand, most of which are out of your control.

Really, now, what is safe and what isn't? Part of the success of many serial killers is that they look so harmless. And what about the spit-polished conservative politician who hugs grandmas and kisses babies, only to turn around and cheat on his wife? Or the clergyman who is also a pedophile? I suppose millions of people have gone for what they thought was the safe choice, only to discover that they stepped into a boiling cauldron of dysfunction.

Which leads me to the conclusion that playing it safe is the greatest risk of all because playing it safe holds the greatest disappointment in store for you if things don't work out. In the ashes of your disaster, you will look back and say, "Wait a minute! I made this choice not because it was my passion, but because I thought it would ensure that a disaster like this wouldn't happen!"

My advice is to thumb your nose at the safe choice and chase your dream, whatever it looks like. Yes, there might be greater risks and a better chance that things won't work out, but at least you'll have the peace that comes from knowing that you went for the big prize in-

stead of settling for the coffee maker. And if it *does* work out, you'll have your dream instead of what feels like a consolation prize.

By the way, I am now married to Travis, which is his real name. I am happy to report that this time I didn't settle. I learned my lesson. You'll get the story of our romance in chapter 11.

making sense of
YOUR *rhythm*

Why playing it safe is the biggest risk of all:

- ✦ Safe is often just a code word for easy.

- ✦ Playing it safe eliminates the possibility that life could surprise you.

- ✦ What appears to be safe might actually be the most dangerous thing of all.

Closing Encouragement

Thumb your nose at the safe choice and chase your dream, whatever it looks like.

God knew better than to tell Noah
that a flood was coming without
telling him how to build the ark.

—Unknown

eight

how is just as important as *why*

I don't make a big deal out of my deafness when I perform. Sometimes, depending on the event, it's not even mentioned, which means that people who don't already know my story can listen to an entire concert and never know that they were listening to a deaf person sing.

In October of 2016 my band and I played the Iridium, a world-class music venue in New York City. It was a thrill for me, especially since the list of performers who have graced that venerable stage reads like a who's who of American music. Les Paul, Steve Miller, Buddy Guy, Joe Walsh, Max Roach, and Michael Brecker are just a few of the legendary artists who have shared their genius under those lights. For a musician, it's like standing on holy ground.

We did two shows, about fourteen songs per show, focusing primarily on our jazz material. After one of the shows, we were approached by four ladies from South America who were vacationing in Manhattan and had set out earlier in the evening to find some live jazz. Because they spoke only Spanish, I couldn't converse with them, but my bass player, Daniel Navarro, who is from Mexico, served as a translator.

"The music was wonderful!" they gushed. "Tell her she has the voice of an angel!"

I thanked them, of course, and stood there uncomprehendingly as they continued to talk with Dan. I noticed that he was shaking his head, responding negatively to whatever it was they were saying. Later, he told me that there was a song they wanted me to sing. He told them I didn't know it and they offered to sing it for me so I could get the tune. Dan said, "That won't work because she's deaf."

As soon as he said that, they looked at me the way they would have if I had just sprouted a third ear. Like most people, it took them a moment or two to process the information. Then, suddenly, they were weeping and hugging me and going on and on in words I couldn't understand. Apparently, their appreciation of our music was exceeded by their amazement that I could pull it off without being able to hear.

This is a very common reaction, and I do understand it. Lots of musicians are blind, and a few are hearing impaired, but almost none are profoundly deaf. Usually, people who hear about me say, "Wait. What did you say? She sings with a band she can't hear? How is that even possible?" In this chapter I want to talk about methodology because it's often the thing that separates people from their dreams.

I'll start with my own methodology, or how I do what I do.

When I lost my hearing, I assumed I was done with music. Who wouldn't? In my mind, my situation was like a sprinter being paralyzed or a marksman losing the ability to see. What I didn't realize is that music was still inside me, bubbling, clamoring to get out, and that my voice, which was no less healthy and strong, gave it an avenue of escape. The only thing missing was a methodology, a way to connect the music inside me with an accompanying instrument. And if I could connect with one instrument, surely I would be able to connect with two or four or even an entire orchestra.

> Music was still inside me, clamoring to get out. The only thing missing was a methodology, a way to connect the music with an instrument.

It helps that I live in a time when there is so much technology because a phone app is at the heart of my methodology. It's a visual tuner that helps me find the first note of a song and make sure I'm not sharp or flat.

I start with middle C. It always amazes people that I have the ability to hit a middle C at any time. If you see me walking down the sidewalk in the middle of rumbling motors and honking horns, and ask me to hit a middle C, I can do it. This is because, when I was in high school, my choir director, Adam Cave, did a lot of ear training with us. I didn't realize what a blessing that would turn out to be. From middle C, I work up or down the scale to find the first note of the song, check with my app to make sure I'm in the dead center of the note, and I'm ready to go.

But of course, finding the pitch and singing the song is only part of the task. I also have to stay with the other musicians, which means staying in tempo and jumping in and dropping out at the right times, which is especially important when performing jazz because improvised solos are so much a part of it. A jazz vocalist might sing the tune one time through and then wait while the instrumentalists play through the form multiple times. In some ways, singing is the easy part; knowing when to sing is the bigger challenge.

This is where I need to take a moment and talk about vibrations.

Sound is all about vibration.

When hearing people listen to music, they are focused on what's happening in their ears. But the fact is that the entire body is picking up vibrations. Scientists tell us that the body is 60 percent water, and water is a great conductor of vibration. Remember the scene from *Jurassic Park* where the coffee and the puddles ripple when the T-rex slams his foot down on the ground? That's what's happening throughout your entire body when sound waves hit you. If you can hear, you have no incentive to pay attention to the vibrations in the rest of your body. But as a deaf person, I do. I focus on vibrations to the point that if someone behind me speaks, I know something was said, not because I heard them in the way that a hearing person would, but because my body picked up the vibration.

This is why some people who don't know me well have accused me of faking my deafness. They see that I react to a sound that happens behind me and say, "Aha! You heard that! You turned around!" They don't understand that I felt the vibrations in my body and knew that something happened behind me.

What I'm describing is why no one should ever use the term "completely deaf." If hearing is all about picking up vibrations, everyone can do that, if not with their ears, then with other parts of their body. Evelyn Glennie, a renowned deaf percussionist who has released more than thirty albums, said in an interview with the BBC: "There's no such thing as total deafness. If the body can feel, that is a form of hearing. Sound is vibration, that's what it is."

> "If the body can feel, that is a form of hearing. Sound is vibration, that's what it is."
>
> —Evelyn Glennie

So back to my performing.

It helps that I have a strong sense of timing. God blessed me by putting a metronome in my head. Still, I have to feel

what the band is doing. I'll never hear it the way you do, but you'd be surprised at what my body "hears." First, I sing barefoot because there's a lot of vibration in the stage floor. If I don't have shoes on, those vibrations come right up through my feet. I also like to position an acoustic bass behind me onstage so that the sound comes through my back and I feel it in my chest. With an electric bass, I feel the vibrations more through the floor. When I first started singing I would place my hand on the piano, which helped me feel the vibrations. Now I've gotten past the need to do that. Basically, my body is being bombarded by rhythmic vibrations when I perform, enabling me to feel the beat and stay in time with the band.

But even that's not all there is to it.

We arrange our songs very specifically, establishing beforehand how long the intro will be, how long the solos will be, where I will reenter after a solo (at the head or the bridge), and what kind of ending we'll put on the tune. This leaves me with a lot of counting to do.

Then again, when you're performing jazz, things don't always go according to plan. Sometimes the musicians get inspired and do something different. This is one of the best things about jazz, but it creates a problem for me. Thankfully, my piano player and I are able to communicate through head nods and facial expressions, enabling me to jump in and out at the right times.

Most of the time.

I'll never forget the night the band got so inspired they modulated up a half step. It was one of those things jazz musicians are prone to do in the excitement of the moment and it almost always sounds great. Except that in this case, I missed the signal and started singing in the same key we'd started the tune in. I knew from the crowd reaction that something was horribly wrong. People were doing the sideways head tilt and scrunching up their faces as if they were in pain. I glanced at the piano player, who realized what had happened. He nodded his head upward and mouthed "go up a half step." I did, and we were suddenly back together.

The upshot of all this is that when I am performing, I am doing a lot more than people in the audience think I'm doing, especially the ones who don't know I'm deaf. They see a girl singing with her band. In truth, I am counting and watching and absorbing sound from head to toe. I also like to sign while I sing, which is often mistaken for some kind of interpretive hand choreography by people who don't realize what I'm doing. They say, "I love what you did with your hands, it was so beautiful!" When I explain that it was sign language, they are surprised.

So I'm counting and watching and absorbing sound and signing and singing during every performance, but that still doesn't cover everything I have to think about onstage. There are still lyrics to remember. Lots and lots of lyrics. Fortunately, I am blessed with a great memory. When I was a kid in grade school and church plays, I always had every kid's part memorized in addition to my own. Again, I had no idea what a blessing that would turn out to be.

All of this is why at the end of a performance I am generally exhausted.

But even all of what I've just mentioned doesn't cover everything that's involved with me doing what I do. There is also the matter of learning songs.

The songs I perform fall into one of three categories: the songs I knew before I lost my hearing, the songs I write, and the new songs I've never heard.

The biggest challenge, as you would expect, is learning a new song I've never heard. First, I have to find the sheet music. Then, using my phone app, I have to find every note in the song and make sure I can "hear" those notes and intervals in my head. To perform confidently, I must concentrate on how the notes feel, the vibrations in my neck and chest and the buzzing in my nasal cavity. I also sit in front of a mirror and pay attention to the movement in my throat as I sing the notes.

When I finally get the notes, I work on the timing. Once I think I'm pretty close to what the song is supposed to sound like, I sing it for someone who coaches me on where I'm a little off. From there I make adjustments until I can sing the song the way it's supposed to go. Then, as we develop an arrangement and I get more comfortable with the song, my knowledge of music theory, which I learned before I lost my hearing, enables me to look at the chords and understand what liberties I can take with the melody.

One of the more interesting aspects of this process is that, having not heard how the original artist does the song, I approach it with no preconceived ideas. All songs start out with me as simple poetry. As I read the lyrics, I sense from the tone and message of the words whether the song should be slow or fast. But I've learned that you can be fooled. Some songs that read like they should be soft and easy are best done up-tempo, and vice versa.

> All songs start out with me as simple poetry.

Sometimes in rehearsal I'll set the tempo for a new tune and the guys will play it through with me. Then one of them will politely say, "Have you thought about doing this tune faster?" Eventually, we nail it down the way it works best.

One more thing about how I perform: I never oversing. It's common, especially among young pop singers, to try to wow the audience with their vocal chops. I'm sure you've noticed how many singers of the national anthem can't just sing the tune but have to turn it into a showcase for their voices, often producing more pyrotechnics than the fireworks display going on behind them. My approach is completely different. I try to respect the song, to pay homage to the composer's intent, to sing in such a way that a person who loves the song won't think that I've ruined it. It's not important to me that people are impressed with my vocal ability; it's important to me that they enjoy the music.

Now let's talk about you.

I often hear it said that *why* you do something is more important than *how*. I don't want to minimize the importance of motivation, but I've noticed that most of the people who make this statement know full well *how* to do what they want to do. They have a strategy laid out and all the tools they need. I suspect that if they had a disability or some other barrier blocking their path, they wouldn't be so quick to minimize the impor-

I try to respect the song, to pay homage to the composer's intent, to sing in such a way that a person who loves the song won't think that I've ruined it.

tance of *how*. In my world, *how* is often the thing standing between people and the fulfillment of their dreams. I wish people would just say that the *why* and the *how* are equally important.

Allow me to offer three suggestions on how to accomplish something that looks like it's going to be really hard.

First, make up your mind that you're willing to accept failure.

A lot of people hold back and never go after their dreams because the thought of failure scares them to death. I had to face this issue the first time I sang at Jay's Bistro, which I talked about earlier in the book. I was terrified that the singing I'd been doing with Dad in our basement wouldn't translate to the stage of a real jazz club. It would have been so easy for me to chicken out at the last minute. I don't think anyone would have blamed me. It wasn't until I decided that I was okay with failing that I found the courage to walk up there and go for it.

I think it's safe to say that creativity and innovation can only happen in an environment where it's okay to fail. Otherwise, you're always holding back, always playing it safe.

Next, if the challenge in front of you looks really hard, simplify it by breaking it down into its component parts.

Most things that appear complicated are actually very simple if you break them down. A guy by the name of Randall Munroe wrote a book called *Thing Explainer*. In this book he takes complicated things and breaks them down, explaining them using no more than a thousand simple words. You can do it with anything.

In my case, I went back to the very basics of music. As I've just shared, to learn a song, I started with the pitches of the notes, then I moved to the time value of the notes, then I added the words. It took hours, but I eventually got it. It would have been impossible for me to walk into a rehearsal and sing through a brand-new song with the band the way a hearing artist would, but by taking the time to break it down and put it back together again, I could get it. I'm confident the challenge in front of you could be broken down, too.

> By taking the time to break it down and put it back together again, I could get it.

But be forewarned! This approach to meeting challenges means that patience must be in your emotional portfolio. Breaking things down and putting them back together is often a slow, tedious process, which probably explains why more people don't achieve their dreams.

Finally, if you're going to tackle a challenge that looks really hard, accept that how you end up doing it may not be how other people do it.

Watch a baseball game and you'll see players with radically differ-ent batting stances.

Talk to authors and you'll find that there are many different ways to write a novel.

Listen to politicians and you'll be reminded that there are differ-ent ways to run a country.

I suppose the only time Ella Fitzgerald sang barefoot was either in the shower or if a new pair of shoes was killing her. For me, barefoot is a must. And while most singers can hear the chord changes and flow with the song without even looking at the musicians, I have to depend on counting measures and head nods to know what comes next. But it's okay! I'm not trying to be Ella (who ever could anyway?). I'm just trying to be the best Mandy I can be.

That should be your goal, too.

Forget trying to be like someone else. Just make up your mind that it's okay if you fail, and then go to work, breaking down your chal-lenge and putting it back together in a way that makes sense for you.

making sense of
YOUR *rhythm*

How to accomplish something that looks really hard.

+ Make up your mind that you're willing to accept failure.

+ If a challenge looks really hard, simplify it by breaking it down into its component parts.

+ Accept that how you end up doing it may not be how other people do it.

Closing Encouragement

Forget trying to be like someone else. Make up your mind that it's okay to fail and then go to work, breaking down your challenge and putting it back together in a way that makes sense for you.

Beware lest you lose the substance by grasping at the shadow.

—Aesop

nine

just because you can't see it doesn't mean it isn't real

s I write these words, the 2016 presidential election is less than a week in the past. It was one of those rare situations where one candidate won the popular vote and the other won the electoral college, and therefore, the presidency. It was merely the final oddity in one of the oddest political seasons in history.

And one of the meanest.

I don't know if we've ever seen so much name-calling and mud-slinging. Vitriol was blown by both candidates like water from a fire hose. And their followers got into the act, too. Normally even-tempered Dr. Jekyll–types morphed into Mr. Hydes, growling and scratching and clawing at anyone from the other side who happened to wander into their bubble. And now, almost a week after the election, we're still seeing riots in the streets.

I mention this not because I intend to go political, but because it's a perfect illustration of a point I want to make in this chapter. Namely, that Americans are not very tolerant and respectful of others.

If you spend any time on Facebook, you know exactly what I mean. Rudeness and vulgarity are the norm. And because social media conversations play out over several days, people feel free to compose long rants that only succeed in provoking the person on the receiving end to hit back a little harder. Many articles have been written about the damage social media is doing to our national mental health.

I feel like an expert on the subject of unkindness in our culture, not because of social media, but because of my disability. I've actually been attacked both verbally and, yes, physically, not because of my politics or skin color, but because of my disability. Who would have imagined that my being deaf would put me in the crosshairs of trigger-happy critics?

Of course, the real problem isn't my disability per se; it's that my disability is invisible. If people could look at me and see that I'm deaf, they'd leave me alone. But because they can't, I am frequently the object of scorn.

Let me give you an example.

If you fly much, you know that it's not unusual for airlines to announce a gate change for a specific flight. The problem for deaf people is that we can't hear those announcements. Yes, there are video screens we can check, but they aren't always within sight and sometimes the gate changes are made at the last minute. On multiple occasions I have missed my flight because I didn't know the departure gate had been changed. To avoid this hardship on disabled passengers, airlines designate a row of handicapped seats near the gate. Airline employees know that if the flight information changes, they must go to the people sitting in those seats and make sure they get the information.

Naturally, when I'm flying alone, I make sure I sit in one of those handicapped seats. But I do so knowing full well that I am going to be at least challenged and maybe attacked simply because I don't look handicapped. I've had people point out to me that I was sitting in a handicapped seat and should move. Others have spoken harshly to me, shaming me for sitting there. Others have reported me to the gate authorities. One guy even poured his Pepsi on me because he thought I was faking a handicap just to get a seat closer to the gate. In an effort to avoid situations like this, I've learned never to speak in airports. I always sign or write things down so people can see that I am deaf.

One guy even poured his Pepsi on me because he thought I was faking a handicap just to get a seat closer to the gate.

At this point, I should say that I do understand where these people are coming from. We *should* be outraged by people who take what belongs to others or try to game the system in some way to gain an advantage. That type of behavior makes me angry, too! My point is simply that before we go into attack mode, we need to make sure we're seeing what we think we're seeing.

Not long ago, some friends invited me to go with them to play golf. I am not a golfer, but I wanted to be with my friends, so I agreed to go along and drive the golf cart. Everything was fine until, on one hole, I pulled up too close to the green. "Back up a little," they said, so I flipped the lever to reverse and rolled back a sufficient distance.

I thought everything was cool.

I was oh-so-wrong.

I didn't know that when you put a golf cart in reverse, it squeals like a banshee and doesn't stop until you take it out of reverse. Which is why a foursome of guys on the next green over stopped their putting and stared at me. Or rather, glared at me. I, of course, was oblivious. The cart I was sitting on was blaring like an air raid siren, and I had no idea.

So the guy who was putting on the next green started shouting at me. What he said, I don't know because I was facing the other way. I only know that my friends started explaining to him that I was deaf and meant no harm. Then they motioned to me to take the cart out of reverse, which I did, though at that moment I was confused as to what was happening.

To the man's credit, he apologized, and I'm sure he felt bad. But it's another example of the unique challenges that are involved in having an invisible disability.

And by the way, there are all kinds of invisible disabilities: PTSD, bipolar disorder, chronic pain (which can cause a variety of illnesses and conditions), depression, epilepsy, chronic fatigue syndrome, and many more. You'd be surprised how many people around you have an invisible disability, or more than one. I, for example, am deaf, but I also suffer from fibromyalgia, connective tissue disease, and deformed Eustachian tubes. Much of my life has been spent battling these things, sometimes all on the same day, though most people who see me walking down the street or even performing would have no idea.

I'm not foolish enough to believe that meanness and rudeness will ever be eliminated, but maybe—just *maybe*—we could lessen it a little by taking the following suggestions seriously.

First, keep in mind that snap judgments are frequently wrong.

Several years ago a study was done of homeless people in a large American city. To the researchers' surprise, a large percentage of them had been to college, had served in the military, or had owned businesses. Readily labeled worthless derelicts by the masses, they were actually educated and often very talented people with impressive accomplishments in their pasts.

There's also the matter of those "panhandlers" you see standing at intersections holding their little handwritten cardboard signs asking for assistance and assuring you they are veterans. An Orlando television station did an investigative report and learned that, again, a surprising percentage of these people are not at all what they seem. Many are, in fact, professional beggars who move around the city from one intersection to another and make astonishing amounts of money. One such person who was interviewed anonymously admitted that he owned a house and a car and became a professional beggar because he could make more money than he was making on his job.

Or think about the married couple who seem so happy . . . until you learn that one of them has had an affair and they're filing for divorce. Or the serial killer who eludes capture, not just by covering his tracks, but by making everyone think he's the nicest guy in the world. Or the beloved pastor whose congregation is devastated to learn of his secret life of sin. I could go on and on. Not a day goes by that people aren't stunned to learn that their impression of someone was sorely mistaken.

The wisest course of action is simply not to make snap judgments. If you see a person sitting in a handicapped chair or parking in a handicapped spot who doesn't look handicapped, tap the brakes and take a deep breath before you charge up to them and start making accusations. If you set yourself up as the disability police, you might be correct in your judgments sometimes, but you'll likely also end up causing a lot of unnecessary pain to people who've already suffered enough.

If you set yourself up as the disability police, you'll likely end up causing a lot of unnecessary pain to people who've already suffered enough.

Second, always make assumptions that favor the handicapped person.

Sadly, we live in a time when it's easy to assume the worst about people. Maybe it's because we know the darkness in our own hearts and assume that other people must be as fallen as we are. Maybe it's because we've all been taken advantage of too many times and have become incurably cynical. Or maybe it's because we've watched too many TV news reports featuring stories about people cheating and scamming the system. As a society, I think we've become jaded. "Nothing surprises me anymore" is a common refrain.

A few years ago at a hospital near where I live, a seventeen-year-old named Matthew Scheidt masqueraded as a doctor (reminiscent of the movie *Catch Me If You Can*), even to the point of wearing scrubs, carrying a stethoscope, and yes, treating patients. At one point, an emergency room physician's assistant walked into a room and saw the teenager using a stethoscope to listen to a patient's breathing while holding an IV catheter in his hand. The physician's assistant assumed the kid was a new doctor he hadn't met yet and turned around and walked out. He later ended up testifying at the imposter's trial and surely made a pact with himself not to be as gullible in the future.

If you know beyond any doubt that a person is faking a disability and, therefore, stealing an opportunity from someone who truly needs it, then yes, sound the alarm. But if you don't know or aren't sure, give the person the benefit of the doubt. Assume that the person has an invisible disability and go on about your business. I believe it's better to allow a scam than to launch an unwarranted attack against a disabled person. The way I figure it, the scam artist will eventually get caught, but the disabled person could be deeply hurt by your unjustified accusation.

Third, don't confuse "doing well" with "being past."

Have you heard of the Invictus Games? They are a multisport competition in which sick and injured armed service personnel and their associated veterans compete in wheelchair basketball, sitting volleyball, and indoor rowing. The name *Invictus* is Latin for "unconquered," and if you could see these athletes compete, you would know it is the perfect name for the games. They are about as far from conquered as you can get. But that doesn't mean they are past their disabilities. If you have no legs, you can have a joyful heart, but a flight

> If you have no legs, you can have a joyful heart, but a flight of stairs still presents a problem.

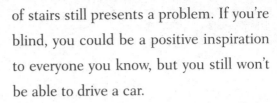

of stairs still presents a problem. If you're blind, you could be a positive inspiration to everyone you know, but you still won't be able to drive a car.

The same is true of invisible disabilities like mine. I am doing well with my inability to hear. I live a happy, productive life by any measure. I have a career that allows me to indulge my passion for music, I travel to all kinds of fun places, and I enjoy the company of many loved ones. But that doesn't mean I have gotten past my disability. The barriers it puts in front of me are sitting there every day when I get out of bed, just waiting to be dealt with.

Most people hear the siren on that approaching emergency vehicle; I don't.

Most people hear the smoke alarm or the oven timer or the doorbell; I don't.

Most people enjoy the music and sound effects in a movie; I don't.

I don't point these things out because I want your pity, but because all disabled people need your understanding. We're never "past" our disabilities; we deal with them every day of our lives. Remembering this may help keep you from saying something insensitive and hurtful.

And here's one more suggestion: Apply these ideas to everyone you meet, not just those who are disabled.

The next person you meet might not have a disability, but he or she will have something that makes life hard; perhaps a difficult parent, a straying spouse, an unreasonable boss, a financial hardship, a sick child, or any one of a hundred other things. Whatever the hardship is might well explain why the person seems quiet, standoffish, irritable, or even sad. Before you criticize, stop and consider that there might be something going on in that person's life that you can't see, something that would fully explain his or her behavior. I'm not suggesting that you should always give the person a pass. It's rarely a good idea to completely ignore bad behavior. But holding off on the snap judgments and giving people the benefit of the doubt is usually a good thing.

What I'm really talking about in this chapter is the importance of not being self-righteous. Most, if not all, of the tendency we have to accuse and criticize comes from the certainty that we're above the thoughtless behavior we see in others. When someone at the airport speaks harshly to me because he thinks I don't belong in a handicapped chair, he's assuring me, at least by implication, that he would never commit such a breach of integrity.

Oh, really?

Did he never plagiarize on a term paper in high school? Has he never eaten a shrimp off his wife's plate at a restaurant that stipulates no sharing? Has he never violated copyright laws by borrowing a friend's CD and burning himself a copy? Has he never let the company expense account pick up the tab for a meal that was only vaguely business related? Has he never double-parked or cut a line or "permanently borrowed" some office supplies from the company supply room?

The problem with being self-righteous is not just that you hurt

> The problem with being self-righteous is not just that you hurt other people, but that you set the bar impossibly high for yourself.

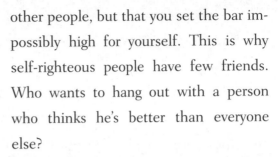

other people, but that you set the bar impossibly high for yourself. This is why self-righteous people have few friends. Who wants to hang out with a person who thinks he's better than everyone else?

My plea is simply that we all dial back our indignation, especially when it comes to people we don't know. If you see someone doing something that doesn't look quite right, don't immediately shift into attack mode. Take a deep breath and consider the possibilities. Are there factors in play that aren't obvious? Could it be that the person is fighting a battle that you're not aware of?

Just because you can't see it doesn't mean it isn't real.

making sense of **YOUR** *rhythm*

Make the world a kinder place by taking the following suggestions seriously:

+ Keep in mind that snap judgments are usually wrong.

+ Always make assumptions that favor the handicapped person.

+ Don't confuse "doing well" with "being past."

+ Apply these ideas to everyone you meet, not just to those who are disabled.

+ Remember, just because you can't see it doesn't mean it's not real.

Closing Encouragement

Take a deep breath and consider the possibilities. Consider that the person is fighting a battle that you're not aware of.

If an exhaustive understanding of God were possible, then God would cease to be God.[10]

—James Emery White

there's no one quite as hurtful as a Christian trying to justify God

When I decided to write this book, I made up my mind that I didn't want it to be overly religious. Yes, I wanted to offer some meaningful life lessons, but I didn't want to come off as some holier-than-thou fanatic because that's not what I am at all. If anyone in this world has a sense of her own shortcomings, it's me. However, I am a Christian, and faith is a huge part of my life. I thank God every day for who he is and for what he's done for me. But my faith has not been without challenges—serious challenges. And no book about my life would be complete without a chapter on the struggles I have faced with regard to my faith. So if talk about faith and God bothers you, you might want to skip ahead to the next chapter.

I'm what some people call a PK, a preacher's kid. While my dad isn't exactly a preacher, he's close enough for me to warrant that designation. Currently a professor at a Christian college, during my middle school and high school years he was an associate pastor in charge of spiritual development at a large church in Colorado.

If you, too, happen to be a preacher's kid, you won't be surprised when I tell you that I was at church pretty much all the time. Every Sunday I was at the church building from 7:00 a.m. until 1:00 p.m. because that's when my parents were there. I was also involved in youth group, helped with the worship team, and went on several mission trips, including four house-building trips to Mexico.

I was baptized at the age of ten by my dad, but not until he sat me down and made sure I understood what I was doing and why. I was not one of those kids who got baptized because my parents wanted me to or because my friends were doing it and I didn't want to be left out. I was sincere in my faith. I loved God and wanted to serve him. And of course I wanted to go to heaven someday.

Because I am an introvert at heart, I've never been one to try to evangelize people. You'll never find me going around asking people if they know they are going to heaven or handing them tracts. However, I do try to witness by example. I've always tried to be the best person I can be. That, together with the fact that I am a preacher's kid, had an effect on how people treated me in high school.

One day in science class, our teacher was talking about evolution and said, "Anyone who doesn't believe in evolution is beyond stupid." Immediately, one of the students said, "You shouldn't say that

A baby photo of Mandy and her older sister, Katie.
MANDY HARVEY

A young Mandy at the pool.
MANDY HARVEY

A Longmont High School dinner theater production.
MANDY HARVEY

A high school choir tour (Mandy is the second to right in the top row) for a competition in Las Vegas, spring 2006.
MANDY HARVEY

Mandy recording her music in high school.
MANDY HARVEY

Mandy behind the scenes in her freshman-year performance in *The Marriage of Figaro*.
MANDY HARVEY

Mandy attending
a deaf social after
her hearing loss.
MANDY HARVEY

Mandy singing and signing at one of her
first conferences in 2009.
GROUP PUBLISHING

The photo for
Mandy's Christmas EP.
KATIE EMRICH

Mandy warming up for a
California performance.
LISA SCHWINGHAMMER

Above and left: Mandy performing in
Beaver Creek, Colorado.
LISA SCHWINGHAMMER

Mandy hiking between performances in Steamboat Springs and Beaver Creek, Colorado.
LISA SCHWINGHAMMER

Mandy's wedding reception.
MANDY HARVFY

Newlyweds in Tennessee, 2012.
MANDY HARVEY

Mandy performing a Christmas concert at Feinstein's/54 Below with deaf composer Jay Alan Zimmerman.
RICK SHEINMEL

Mandy performing in 2016 with her ukulele at a charity event in Naples, Florida.
RON McGINTY

Mandy performing at the 2016 No Barriers Summit in Copper Mountain, Colorado.
NO BARRIERS USA

Mandy with Miami's *The Rebound* team at the 2016 No Barriers Summit in Copper Mountain, Colorado.
SHAINA KOREN

WWW.REBOUNDTHEFILM.COM

Mandy leading worship at Real Life Church on Easter 2017.
REAL LIFE CHURCH

Mandy singing and signing "Smile," the song that Charlie Chaplin made famous.
MATT SALACUSE/DEVON DAY REPS

in front of Mandy." Everyone snickered, of course, and I did a slow burn, though I didn't let on that it upset me. If I had, they would have poured it on even more. That kind of thing happened a lot.

Which brings me to the start of my college career.

Little did I know when I started classes at Colorado State University that my circumstances and my faith were on a collision course.

On the very first day of the fall semester, I ran into some students I knew from a mission trip I'd gone on. We were happy to see each other, and they immediately invited me to come to their church and join a weekly Bible study for college students. I thought that sounded good, especially since I wasn't going home most weekends, so I did.

Not long after that, I started losing my hearing.

Because it happened gradually, and because there seemed to be options that could help me (like hearing aids), I spent the first semester scared and worried, but with at least some hope. It wasn't until I got into the second semester and realized the hearing aids weren't working that I knew I was in real trouble. And here's the point: What should have been a time of leaning on my church friends for support became just the opposite. Of all the people in my life, they were the ones I hated being around the most.

What should have been a time of leaning on my church friends for support became just the opposite.

It started when they came to my room one day to have a talk with me. They'd noticed that I was quiet at Bible study and knew what I was going through with my ears, so they felt the need to impart some

wisdom on me, which was this: "You can't let yourself become angry at God. Remember, if you have enough faith, God will heal you."

Boom!

That sound you just heard was the massive pile of guilt they dropped squarely on top of my head.

Remember, Mandy, if you have enough faith, God will heal you.

The logical extension of that statement is: *if you don't have enough faith, you get to go on being deaf.* Meaning, of course, that it's all on my shoulders. If I don't get a miracle of healing it's because God has judged my faith to be unworthy of his favor.

I've now had a lot of time to process this statement. I now understand that they were desperate to try to justify God. My hearing loss didn't fit with their image of a God who loves to bless people with good times, health, and prosperity. Simply put, it blew a gaping hole in their theology. So their only option was to lay the blame for my situation on me. If I'm deaf, I have only myself to blame because my faith is too weak.

> My hearing loss didn't fit with their image of a God who loves to bless people with good times, health, and prosperity.

If they had only said this once, I might have been able to weather it. But it became their theme. Every time I ran into one of them, they reminded me of all the wonderful things God was ready to do for me . . . if only my faith was strong enough.

Let me say very clearly that I don't think they were trying to be mean. But honestly, a punch in the gut would have felt better. Imagine a woman losing her marriage. She discovers that her husband is

seeing someone else and preparing to file for divorce, and then someone comes along and says, "If you're a good enough wife, God will
give you your husband back." What do you even do with a statement
like that? Especially if you feel you've always tried to be the best wife
you can be? That's where I was. I had always taken my faith seriously.
I tried my best to behave. I never smoked or drank or chased boys.
And as for prayer, as my hearing loss progressed, I prayed until I had
no more words. I humbly sought God's will and purpose for my life.
And suddenly I'm being told that my dreams are crashing and burning
because I don't have enough faith?

Another aspect of this situation is that the people who were doing
this to me had the reputation of being strong, mature Christians. You
find people like this in every church. Some people call them the "pil-
lars" or the "backbone" of the church. They're the people with the
aura, the glow of spirituality that causes others to be just a little bit
in awe. I admit that I was just that when I first started attending their
Bible study. So it was hard for me to process how these super-spiritual
people could now be my biggest source of emotional pain.

Rock bottom for me came one night when I was reading my Bible.

A few years earlier, I had attended a Christ in Youth conference,
which is geared for teens. One of my assignments at that conference
was to think about what my biggest fear was and to write down a plan
for how to deal with it if it ever happened. Because of the countless
problems I've had with my ears, mostly relating to my deformed Eustachian tubes, my biggest fear had always been that I would lose my
hearing. So I obediently wrote out a plan for what I would do if that
ever happened.

The plan wasn't too deep or original, probably typical of what a high schooler would come up with. I said that I would pray a lot and trust God to get me through it. I also found a short Bible passage that would guide me through. It was Romans 5:2–4: "We boast in the hope of the glory of God. Not only so, but we also glory in our sufferings, because we know that suffering produces perseverance; perseverance, character; and character, hope."

So one night four years later, while in the middle of a spiritual crisis the likes of which I had never known, I actually found this assignment folded up and stuck in the back of my Bible. I hadn't seen it or thought about it in years. When I unfolded it and started to read, I felt that it was mocking me. I had promised to pray and trust God, but now I was being told that it was my lack of faith that was preventing me from being healed. That very night I burned that piece of paper. I couldn't bear to have it anywhere near me.

What I've just shared with you had a major impact on my life. I spent months alternating between anger and deep depression, not able to pray or read my Bible, and feeling completely unworthy in every way. Becoming deaf was bad enough, but the thought that it was my fault God wasn't healing me was just more than I could take.

And then one day I came to a turning point.

I'd had lots of conversations with people who loved and wanted to help. My dad, for example, kept telling me that I didn't need to think in terms of whys or what-ifs, I just needed to stay on the path of faithfulness. I appreciated all the attempts to encourage me, but none of the advice came together in my mind until one day when I fell down some stairs. It was pure clumsiness on my part. I simply missed a step and the next thing I knew, I was sprawled on the floor.

I wasn't seriously injured, but I was hurt badly enough that a helping hand would have been nice. However, there was no one home, so I sat there contemplating my situation. And it was in that moment that I had an epiphany. I suddenly understood that pain is a reality in life, not just for me, but for everybody. But it's the response to pain that ultimately tells the story of a person's life. In other words, everybody falls, but not everybody gets up. I knew in my heart that I had fallen, spiritually. (Or perhaps I was pushed by my Bible study friends, I don't know.) And now it was time for me to quit moping and get up. So as I pushed my aching bones off the floor that day, I was getting up in more ways than one. I won't say that I was suddenly, magically transformed, but I will say that it was the start

> It's the response to pain that ultimately tells the story of a person's life. In other words, everybody falls, but not everybody gets up.

of my comeback. In fact, I was so surprised, encouraged, and hopeful in that moment that I actually laughed.

At this point I want to stop and say some things to those of you who are well-meaning people of faith. These are realities we would all do well to remember.

To begin with, our faith should be a blessing to people, not a club we use to beat them up.

I don't want to be overly harsh, but my Bible study peers (I can't call them friends) "bludgeoned" me with their faith. I'm sure it was unintentional, but so what? If I run over someone and make him a paraplegic, I can say, "Oh, I'm sorry, I didn't mean to do that," but he will still be paralyzed. As Christians, we need to check ourselves to make sure that, in our zeal, we're not causing pain.

As was the case in my situation, much of the pain Christians cause is the result of thoughtless comments. And by thoughtless, I mean comments that come flying out of our mouths before we think about how they're going to feel to the person on the receiving end.

To a hurting person, "If you have enough faith, God will heal you" sounds like "If you still have this ailment, it must be your fault."

> To a hurting person, "If you have enough faith, God will heal you" sounds like "If you still have this ailment, it must be your fault."

To a hurting person, "If God isn't answering your prayers, there must be sin in your life" sounds like "You deserve everything that's happening to you, you sinner."

To a hurting person, "God must be trying to teach you something through this suffering" sounds like "If you weren't so stupid, God wouldn't have to teach you things the hard way."

And in reality, cliché-heavy statements like these are eaten through with bad theology. But I'll leave that one for the Bible scholars. My point is simply that we ought to be very careful what we say to hurting people.

Second, rather than saying, "Here's what your problem is," say, "How can I help you?"

The thing I noticed about my Bible study peers is that they were very quick to pontificate about the shortcomings of my faith, but they never came along beside me and offered to walk with me through the darkness. Their response had no "ministry" component. They were quick to tell me what my problem was, but they never offered their help or support.

They said, "Here's what your problem is," but they never said, "How can we help you?"

If there's one thing I've learned on my uphill journey, it's that actions are more precious than words. A helping hand is worth ten times as much as a nugget of theology. This is why the Bible says, "Faith without deeds is dead" (James 2:14–26).

Next, any theology that presumes to answer every question is a flawed theology.

Some questions are simply unanswerable, such as why a college freshman music major who loves God suddenly began to lose her hearing. The only honest answer to that question is "I have no idea." But when your theology can't accommodate unanswerable questions, you have to come up with something, even if it's hurtful and damaging. "If you have enough faith, God will heal you" allows the speaker to breathe a sigh of relief because he avoided saying the dreaded "I don't know." But it feels like a kidney punch to the sufferer.

Why can't we just admit that there are things we don't understand? Do we feel that we're somehow letting God down? On the contrary! Acknowledging that God's ways are more mysterious than we can ever hope to grasp is actually a compliment to him. Think about

> Acknowledging that God's ways are more mysterious than we can ever hope to grasp is actually a compliment to him.

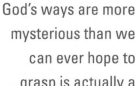

it. How pitiful would God have to be for us to understand all his ways?

Oh, how I wish my Bible study peers would have simply said, "We don't know why you're going through this, but we love you and we're praying for you, and if you ever need anything, we'll be here for you." It seems so simple, but it must be very hard, judging by the number of believers who have no idea what to say to a hurting person. So I must offer this final suggestion, though it sincerely pains me to say it:

Sometimes it's best to step away from a particular community of faith and look for a different one.

I am a strong believer in Christian fellowship. I've been the beneficiary of it on countless occasions. But not all communities are created equal. Some are healthy and some are toxic. Some are edifying and some are oppressive. That goes for churches and small groups alike. Allow me to draw some distinctions between the two extremes.

Healthy fellowships continually seek truth, while toxic ones feel they already have all the answers.

Healthy fellowships accept that some questions are unanswerable, while toxic ones feel they must come up with an answer to every question.

Healthy fellowships do a lot of serving and very little lecturing, while toxic ones do a lot of lecturing and very little serving.

Healthy fellowships immediately embrace broken people, while toxic ones immediately try to fix them.

Healthy fellowships send you home feeling increased, while toxic ones send you home feeling diminished.

Toxic fellowships are in the minority, but there are enough of them out there that you could find yourself a part of one someday. If it ever happens, it's vitally important that you step away and find one that can edify you, for after glorifying God, that is the ultimate goal of any group of believers. 1 Thessalonians 5:11 says, "Therefore encourage one another and build each other up."

To close, let me just say that my spiritual struggles, while incredibly painful and difficult at times, have left me a better, stronger, and wiser person. In fact, I now respond differently than I used to when I'm asked a certain question that comes my way quite often. People say, "How's the world treating you?" My answer has finally become what I believe to be the right one: "The world is indifferent to me, but God is good."

making sense of
YOUR *rhythm*

When sharing your faith with a person who's hurting, remember these things:

✦ Make sure your faith blesses rather than harms.

✦ Rather than saying "This is what your problem is," ask "How can I help?"

✦ A theology that presumes it can answer every question is a flawed theology.

✦ There may come a time when it's best to step away from a particular community of faith and look for a different one.

Closing Encouragement

Be the person who says, "I don't know why you're going through this, but I love you and I'm praying for you, and if you ever need anything, I'll be here for you."

Look closely at the present you are constructing. It should look like the future you are dreaming.[11]

—Alice Walker

eleven

there is power in *replacement*

*T*his chapter is very special to me. I'm going to talk about something that has dramatically changed my life. Something I believe will work for everyone.

To do that, it's necessary for me to bring back You-Know-Who. If you don't know who You-Know-Who is, that means you skipped chapter 7. If you'd like to stop right here and go back and read that chapter, you'll be better prepared to understand this chapter.

Go ahead, I'll wait.

———————

So now you know that You-Know-Who is my first husband. Otherwise referred to by my family as Voldemort, of Harry Potter fame—the guy whose name we never speak.

On Saturday, May 29, 2010, at 10:30 in the morning, I married him. As far as bad choices go, it was epic. I won't rehash the content of chapter 7 (heaven knows, once is enough!), but I do want to nail down a few facts that will be pertinent for what follows.

One is that it was my first relationship. I'd never been in love before and was excited to finally be experiencing what so many of my friends had already experienced. Perhaps that's why I ignored so many red flags. I didn't want to lose what it took me so long to find, and what I was afraid I might never find again. Keep in mind, when you're deaf, it's not as easy to mix and mingle and get to know people. And there is a certain percentage of people who simply don't want to be in a relationship with a handicapped person.

The biggest reason for the whole debacle is me, not my ex. I'm referring to those red flags I ignored.

A second pertinent fact is that the biggest reason for the whole debacle is me, not my ex. No, I was never unfaithful or anything like that. I'm referring to those red flags I ignored. On more than one occasion I took off my ring, determined to end the relationship. The frustrations were practically unbearable. But every time this happened, he would say the things I needed to hear, and I would put the ring back on and try again. That's not on him, it's on me. I look back and wonder what on earth I was thinking.

The third and most pertinent fact is that I came out of that relationship with a lot of bad memories of specific times and places that became particularly oppressive to me. Let me give you an example.

Chipotle is my favorite restaurant, and not just because I love the food. It was where I went with my friends in high school, a place where we laughed and talked about whatever drama was going on in our lives. Kids in the *Happy Days* era had their malt shops and diners. We had Chipotle. Then when You-Know-Who and I started hanging out, it became our place to go and hash out the day's events. He loved it as much as I did.

So naturally, it didn't surprise me one day when he asked me to meet him there. This was a few months into our marriage. Things weren't going well, and he had actually moved out of our apartment, but I didn't think our problems were insurmountable. I told myself that with a few adjustments we'd be fine. Little did I know that he was going to tell me he wanted a divorce right there in Chipotle, of all places. Something like that should be done in private, but no, he chose a public place, and one where I had built up so many wonderful memories. Not only did he tell me he was going to divorce me, he asked me to give him my engagement ring so he could pawn it and pay some bills. This was even more of a slap in the face than you might think because I actually paid for the ring myself.

That was the last time we were in Chipotle together. Friends told me that he continued to go there. They said they saw him there with other girls, which only served to further contaminate the place in my mind. What had once been one of my favorite places in the world suddenly became a place I couldn't stand to drive past, let alone walk into. It was like a pure mountain stream that had been poisoned by toxic chemicals.

But it wasn't just Chipotle. There were other places, such as a curve on Route 287 going from Longmont to Loveland. It's the spot where You-Know-Who pulled over one day and asked me to marry him. After our marriage fell apart, I found it difficult to drive past that spot without feeling overwhelmed by negative emotions. I felt disappointed and angry. Most of all, I felt foolish for saying yes to his proposal. It was as if that curve marked the spot where I made the worst decision of my life. It seemed to call out to me, to make fun of me as I drove by.

My point is that there were quite a few of these places that triggered emotional reactions in me. Places that seemed to mock me. Places that made me feel either sick or furious or both. Places I began to avoid at all costs.

I'm not a psychologist, but I know this sort of thing is very unhealthy. It's important to understand the impact and significance of our bad experiences and to learn what we can from them. But when we allow them to shape our thinking and behavior in ways that diminish us, something is wrong. I was being diminished by the feeling that I had to stay away from places and people that had once meant a lot to me. It was as if someone had taken my scrapbook of beautiful memories and scribbled over the pages with a black Sharpie.

> When we allow bad experiences to shape our thinking and behavior in ways that diminish us, something is wrong.

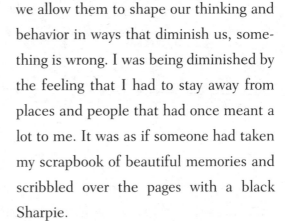

Enter a man named Travis.

We started dating in 2011. I noticed right away that we had a different vibe. As our relationship deepened, we both sensed that we had something special. When Travis proposed, I said yes, but we agreed to wait one full year. I was determined to be smarter this time, to be on the lookout for red flags. And to pay attention to them.

Want to hear something odd? Travis and I were married on May 4, 2012, the exact one-year anniversary of my divorce from You-Know-Who. I only discovered this when I was applying for a marriage license. They asked for the date of my divorce and I didn't know it. I knew when the papers were filed and signed, and I remember being notified that it was official, but as for the exact day, I had no idea. It was only when I obtained the paperwork that I realized the wedding day Travis and I chose was exactly one year to the day after my divorce was final.

Obviously, Travis knew that I was carrying painful memories, that I was avoiding certain places. He also understood how unhealthy it is to let painful memories control you. So he challenged me to join him on a mission. We would go to all the places where I had painful memories and replace them with positive ones.

For example, we went to that curve on Route 287. You aren't supposed to pull over there, but You-Know-Who did when he proposed, so Travis did, too. We got out of the car and walked around and talked about our love for each other. He even kissed me as cars were zooming by. Those drivers must have thought we were starry-eyed lovers who couldn't control our passion. I wish they could have known that we were exorcising a demon. From that point on, the curve on 287 became a special place that held a beautiful memory.

We also made a road trip to Montana to replace an unpleasant trip I had made with You-Know-Who. We went to Boulder, a place I had avoided because You-Know-Who lived there. And yes, we chased the ghosts out of Chipotle and turned it back into the happy place it once was. We knocked down one painful memory after another, like dominoes falling in a chain reaction. And the way we did it was by *replacing* the old ugliness with new, beautiful experiences.

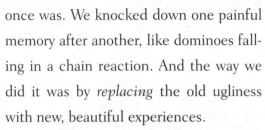

> We knocked down one painful memory after another by *replacing* the old ugliness with new, beautiful experiences.

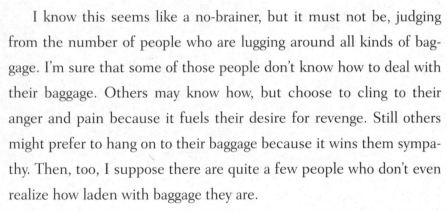

With all of that in mind, let me share some thoughts about unhealthy baggage.

First and foremost: that baggage needs to be shed.

I know this seems like a no-brainer, but it must not be, judging from the number of people who are lugging around all kinds of baggage. I'm sure that some of those people don't know how to deal with their baggage. Others may know how, but choose to cling to their anger and pain because it fuels their desire for revenge. Still others might prefer to hang on to their baggage because it wins them sympathy. Then, too, I suppose there are quite a few people who don't even realize how laden with baggage they are.

Here's the problem with toting unhealthy baggage as you go through life: It boxes you in. It traps you in a cage with your bad experiences. It says, "This is where you must live from now on. Everything you say and do must in some way relate to what happened. Every person you meet and every opportunity that comes your way must be viewed through the lens of your pain." This is how our baggage diminishes us.

I've known people, and I'm sure you have, too, who are so trapped inside their pain that they are unable to have normal relationships with their family members or coworkers. You have to walk on eggshells around them, avoid certain topics, and tolerate their anger-fueled comments. Above all, you try to avoid getting stuck in their company. You don't want to ride with them or sit next to them or socialize with them on the weekends.

When I talk about shedding baggage, I'm really talking about being set free.

So when I talk about shedding baggage, I'm really talking about being set free. I love to fish and I'm always struck by how a fish reacts when it's been caught and is released back into the water. There may be a brief instant when it doesn't realize it's free, but as soon as it does, it's gone like a bullet shot from a gun, speeding off toward the safety of the deep, thrilled to no longer be trapped. People can have that experience, too.

Second, we all have baggage to deal with, but there are some really wrong ways of dealing that we need to avoid.

One of those ways is denial.

Most people who are carrying baggage might as well have a flashing neon sign around their necks announcing the fact. All it takes is a date or two, or a couple of days working beside them, and you know they're lugging a load. Baggage is about as easy to hide as a nine-month pregnancy, but people try, mostly because of pride. We believe that if people find out about our baggage, they'll follow the breadcrumb trail back to its source—often our poor choices or bad be-havior—and lose respect for us. It never occurs to us that people are more apt to lose respect for us for living in denial than for any mis-takes we've made. *Everybody* has made mistakes!

Another wrong way to deal with baggage is by numbing yourself.

Your first thought here might be of drugs or alcohol, but don't overlook the numbing effects of TV or social media or binge shopping or an affair or even an eighty-hour workweek. Any excessive behavior that keeps you from thinking about your baggage will seem enticing, but will only open up a whole new set of problems in the long run.

One more common and very unhealthy way to deal with baggage is by allowing it to fuel your anger.

Perhaps you've known a woman who was abused by a man, so now she hates all men and never misses an opportunity to spew venom to-ward them. Or maybe you had a bad experience in church, so now you refuse to go and tell everyone you meet that all churchgoers are hypocrites. Sometimes it goes even further than words. Daily reports about domestic violence, workplace violence, road rage, and all kinds of other horrific encounters are a constant reminder of how many truly angry people are walking our streets. You can be sure a lot of that anger is being fueled by baggage.

I'm convinced that dealing with baggage the wrong way is just as bad as—if not worse than—not dealing with it at all.

Finally, there is a healthy way to deal with baggage.

When Travis and I began replacing my bad experiences with good ones, we were actually accomplishing a couple of things. First, we were identifying my baggage, not just in some vague, psychobabble kind of way, but very specifically: *I can't go to Chipotle because the memory of that horrible moment when I learned my marriage was officially dead haunts me.* You can't get much more specific than that. Hence, we knew exactly what we needed to work on. Second, we were attacking the problem head-on. You'll hear people say that time heals all wounds. While time does indeed have healing properties, it's not a cure-all. Some people are still waiting for time to heal their wounds decades after the wounds were inflicted. Travis and I chose to be proactive, to chase down the healing I needed rather than let it find its way to us, which it might never have done on its own.

Another aspect of our replacement strategy that deserves mentioning is that it was something we had to work on together. Whereas You-Know-Who and I always seemed disconnected on multiple levels, Travis and I were suddenly working together as a team. That alone made me feel wonderful. It affirmed my belief that this time around things were going to be different.

Looking back, I realize that I could've opted for counseling. I could have spent weeks or months pouring my pain out to a doctor in one-hour increments. And it might have helped. I am a firm believer in counseling. But, for me, the replacement idea seemed more intriguing and less intimidating. It was something Travis could help me with. And it was something we could work on as we saw fit, rather than being confined to one-hour weekly appointments. Also, there's something to be said for activity. Sometimes I think there's too much talking and not enough doing in the world.

When you replace a painful experience with a positive one, you're making a powerful statement: *I am not a slave to what happened.* It

When you replace a painful experience with a positive one, you're making a powerful statement: *I am not a slave to what happened.*

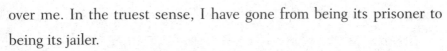

doesn't mean you won't remember what happened. You *need* to remember it to help ensure it doesn't happen again. But it does mean you're not going to let that experience be the end of your story.

Today, when I go to Chipotle, I don't break out in a sweat or have flashbacks to one of the worst moments of my life. That memory no longer holds any power over me. In the truest sense, I have gone from being its prisoner to being its jailer.

making sense of YOUR *rhythm*

Some thoughts about unhealthy "baggage":

+ First and foremost: unhealthy baggage needs to be *shed*!

+ Be mindful of how you deal with baggage: denying it or numbing yourself or allowing it to fuel your anger only leads to more pain.

+ Replacing a painful experience with a positive one says to you and the world, "I am no longer a slave to what happened. I am free!"

Closing Encouragement

In the truest sense, you can go from being a prisoner of your painful memories to being their jailer.

The bumps are what you climb on.[12]

—Warren Wiersbe

twelve

pain is a friend
masquerading as a monster

You know about my hearing loss. I'd love to tell you that it's been the primary source of pain in my life, but that wouldn't be true. Quite a while before I lost my hearing, I suffered a physical trauma that turned into a nightmare.

It all started in high school PE. We were doing our warm-up, which consisted of jogging around the gym. People say that in life's most significant moments, time slows down, that you remember everything happening around you, that you seem to watch what's happening to yourself. For me, it was the opposite. Time sped up. I was running and laughing, and then I was on the floor. I don't remember stepping down awkwardly. I don't remember anything buckling. I didn't hear a snap or a crack.

One of my friends had reached out and pushed my shoulder. It wasn't anything malicious. We'd been laughing and joking, and she was simply reacting to something I had said. It was the kind of thing that happens in PE classes all across America every single day.

Not wanting to be a danger to the other runners who were stampeding toward me from behind, I quickly crawled out of the way. Most of the runners passed me by. A few looked back. A couple stopped.

The friend who had unintentionally pushed me down stopped, of course, and was standing there, staring at me. She had lost all the color in her face. When I asked her to go get the coach, it was as if she were doing the Mannequin Challenge. I had to scream at her to bring her back to reality.

The coach arrived with the assumption that I had rolled my ankle, a common-enough PE injury. It didn't take but a second for him to see that the problem was my knee. When he moved my leg slightly, I experienced pain that was so intense it made me nauseous. I've heard people talk about pain that stabs like a knife. This wasn't like that. It was a deep, all-encompassing pain, the kind that reverberated from head to toe.

When he moved my leg slightly, I experienced pain that was so intense it made me nauseous.

Coaches aren't doctors, but most of them have seen quite a few sports-related injuries, so they have a sense of what's serious and what isn't. When my coach saw my knee, he looked startled, which was not encouraging to me. He said, "Okay, we're going to call your parents. We're going to call the nurse. We're going to get some people down here."

As I lay there on the floor staring at the ceiling, awful fears were running through my head: I thought about how many surgeries I might be facing and if I would ever be able to walk normally again. Or if I would be able to walk at all.

People were talking all around me. Not to me, but to one another, discussing how best to get me out of the gym, whether or not to call an ambulance, whether or not to wait for my parents and let them make the decision. It was weird, lying there as helpless as a bag of mulch while other people decided my fate.

When I turned my head and saw my parents coming toward me, I lost it. When they knelt beside me, I said, "I'm so sorry. This is going to cost a lot of money." They said, "No, don't worry about that." But I couldn't help it.

Mom drove me to a local clinic where I was laid on a table, all stretched out with my head on a pillow. Amazingly, the pain disappeared. I can't say why. Maybe when I had been in a sitting position on the gym floor I was stretching and pulling things in my leg. All I know is that, lying on that table, I felt a rush of euphoria because nothing hurt. My shakes even stopped. Tears were flowing down my cheeks, but I wasn't actually crying. I think my body was just trying to release the tension.

Finally, a doctor, an older gentleman, came in to have a look. A five-year-old playing Doc McStuffins could have seen my knee was dislocated. He said that one option was to try to relocate it right then and there. We discussed this and decided it was worth a shot.

Relocating a dislocated joint without anesthesia is horrifying. My mom actually lay across the top of me to keep me from flying off the table from sheer rage as the doctor manipulated my knee. The nurses, who had to have been accustomed to painful medical procedures, were crying. My emotions at that moment are hard to describe. To say that I contemplated murder would not be a stretch. If I could have found anything within my reach to throw at or stab the person causing my pain, I think I would have done it. I'd never felt the kind of pain that causes murderous rage before, and I hope I never do again.

This went on for several minutes. Finally, the doctor gave up and decided to send me to the hospital, where I would be put under and have my knee relocated while I was asleep. In no time I was on a gurney, covered in warm blankets, and being transported across town in an ambulance.

After the relocation that got me through the original trauma, the doctors informed my parents and me that I would need reconstructive surgery. Apparently my kneecap was about the only thing that was where it was supposed to be. Everything else was ripped or ruptured and now located in a place where it didn't belong. However, the reconstructive surgery wouldn't be performed for at least two weeks to give the swelling a chance to go down.

> To say that I contemplated murder would not be a stretch.

To prevent further damage while I waited for surgery, my right leg was put in a hard plaster cast from hip to toe. And it was surprisingly heavy, weighing about thirty pounds.

As a result, there were things I simply couldn't do, like get myself out of bed or walk from wherever I was to the bathroom.

I tried to hobble with a walker, but I didn't have the strength. So in true necessity-is-the-mother-of-invention style, my mom came up with an ingenious plan. We attached a dog leash to my plaster-encased ankle. Mom would hold the other end of the leash and pull

In true necessity-is-the-mother-of-invention style, my mom came up with an ingenious plan.

my leg forward, forcing my leg to take a "step." Then I would step forward with my good leg while moving the walker forward.

Pull.

Step.

Move the walker forward.

Pull.

Step.

Move the walker forward.

We didn't set any land speed records, but the system worked pretty well. Then, of course, there was the problem of how to deal with the bathroom after I finally got there. Getting my pants down over a thirty-pound cast that came all the way up to my hip, not to mention actually sitting down on the toilet with the cast and a stiff leg, required quite a feat of engineering. Let me just say that I became quite good at peeing sideways. Then I would call for help. Mom would come running and hoist me up. After pulling up and repositioning my underwear, we would head back down the hall:

Pull.

Step.

Move the walker forward.

I learned a lot about humility in those days following the injury. I came to appreciate how much my family loves me and how blessed I am to have them in my life. Mom helped me get back and forth to the bathroom and helped me bathe. Sammi and Josh made sure my Cryopak, which helped with pain and inflammation, never ran out of ice. Dad and a family friend built a wheelchair ramp to our front door. You may see your family every day, but in moments like these you see your family for who they really are and for who you are to them. I have never felt more loved. They couldn't take away my pain, but they were willing to sacrifice anything they could to help me carry it.

They couldn't take away my pain, but they were willing to sacrifice anything they could to help me carry it.

I'm tempted to say that I spent the next two weeks lying in bed doing nothing, but that's not exactly true. I watched a lot of movies, mastered the art of sideways peeing, and spent a lot of time being angry. Other than *that*, I did nothing.

Finally, I got the call.

My surgery would be at Boulder Community Hospital. And the surgeon would replace all four of my ligaments and do some other repair work. And . . . I was going to have *bone screws* inserted in my leg. The sound of that just makes you want to wince, doesn't it? Archimedes is said to have invented the screw in the third century BC. I doubt that he foresaw this application for the little devils.

The process started, as always, with an IV, which required multiple sticks. Then came what they called "happy drugs," which failed to deliver anything resembling happiness. Even though I was supposed to be "fading," I was still aware of everything—including the tools they were about to use on me. Surgical tools are often used in horror films for a reason. They looked like what you would use to build a cruise ship. Or cut one apart.

And it was *cold* in the operating room. Freakishly cold. So cold that I started shaking. Someone covered me up with some warm blankets, which I appreciated. Then they asked me to start counting backward from a hundred. Most people who start this countdown don't remember ninety-five. I was still going strong well into the eighties. No one remembers the last number they count, and I don't either, but I know I lasted longer than I was supposed to.

But then during the surgery, I began to feel things happening to my leg. I heard people talking, though I didn't understand what they were saying. It was all very syrupy.

Suddenly, I felt them switching my IV from one hand to the other. This is not something you are supposed to be able to feel while under anesthesia. Through the fog, I said, "Why are you moving my IV?" This set off quite a reaction from the people who were working on me. I heard a gasp. I sensed a lot of sudden movement. Then I floated away again.

Later, I learned that the meds weren't affecting me like they do most people. They were giving me enough to knock out a horse, but I wasn't staying under. That's why they thought something was wrong with the IV and decided to try a new one in the other arm.

When I next opened my eyes, I was in the recovery room with a

headache like I'd never had before. And there were still bigger problems to come.

My body refused to respond to the pain medication I was being
given. The medication that was supposed to soothe and relax me had
no effect whatsoever. If anything, the pain got worse. So they cranked
it up a notch or two, but still I felt no results. So they tried different
medications, then multiple medications, all to no effect. Not only did the wound from my surgery hurt, I also felt intense heat all over, like my body was on fire.

The medication that was supposed to soothe and relax me had no effect whatsoever.

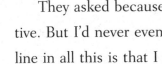

During this time, the medical staff started questioning me.

"Are you or have you ever abused drugs?"

They asked because drug abuse often renders pain meds ineffec-
tive. But I'd never even seen illegal drugs except on TV. The bottom
line in all this is that I was suddenly confronted with one cold, hard
truth: I was going to go through rehab without anything to take the
pain away.

The only thing that truly helped deaden my pain was a Cryopak.
Cryotherapy is all about using cold temperature to treat an injured
part of the body. In my case, my leg was put into a sleeve that had ice
water circulating through it. At first, I felt a burning sensation from
the cold, but the longer it was on, the better it felt until I can honestly say it felt amazingly good. But when the ice melted, the pain
returned, so I did not hesitate to call for more ice. The motor that cir-

culated the water through my Cryopak was obnoxiously loud. Even so, it became my best friend.

Before long I was put into a Continuous Passive Motion (CPM) machine. It's simply a machine that forces your leg to bend. People who have joint surgeries don't want to move their limbs, and understandably so. The pain is intense. But this machine doesn't care. Once your leg is strapped in, it's going to bend. The bending is slow and controlled, and the range of motion is usually increased over time. The idea is to prevent the limb from becoming locked up and unusable.

When I finally got home from the hospital, another challenge reared its ugly head. This time it was my emotions that came under attack. I just had a terrible time dealing with life.

Going to the bathroom became such a challenge once again that I often broke down halfway there and wanted to give up. And I knew this wasn't me. I could understand being sad and frustrated—anybody in my situation would be—but I had never been such an emotional wreck.

With my mom's help, I began to understand that a lot of it was the medication. It wasn't helping me with the pain the way it was supposed to, but it was messing with my emotions. So we decided to sleep off the medication and see how I felt without it. I went to bed and slept for hours. When I woke up I was in intense pain, but at least I felt like the real me emotionally. That's when I came to the conclusion that my first priority from that point forward would be to feel like myself. Somehow I would deal with the pain as long as I could be me.

My first priority became to feel like myself. Somehow I would deal with the pain as long as I could be me.

Part of my strategy for "being me" was to keep up with my music. It was something I loved and something I could control to some degree. Yes, I was missing out on things at school, but I could make music right there in my bed by turning two buckets upside down on either side of me and then laying a keyboard across them. I could play and sing, not just to distract myself, but also to keep something I loved in my life when so many other things had been taken away.

Once again, my parents were an immense support. Similar to my struggles before my surgery in that huge cast, I couldn't bathe myself or get dressed, and I again needed help in the bathroom. These are things parents delight in helping their toddler children with, but there's a kind of sadness to it when children are approaching adulthood and need that kind of help. It was hard for them because it goes so strongly against the natural order of things. Even so, my parents were always there for me.

One of the many things my dad did was build a ramp so we could get the wheelchair in and out of the house. He had it ready for me when I got home from the hospital.

As part of my recovery, the doctor wanted my knee to be able to bend up to and beyond a forty-five-degree angle, but even with the physical therapy and the CPM machine, we hadn't gotten there. The recommendation was to force it.

I'll never forget the day I sat in a dining room chair and my mom sat on the floor, pushing on my leg, trying to force it past forty-five degrees. I hated her in that moment. I don't know how else to say it. The pain was indescribable, and my screams bounced off the walls; but she kept pushing, trying to break through the scar tissue. I remember thinking that she might be enjoying the moment, that it was a way for her to get back at me for all the times I had disobeyed her during my childhood. It was a ridiculous thought, of course. My mom would have given anything not to have had to live that moment with me. In some ways, pushing on my knee probably hurt her more than it did me. It occurs to me now that my mom loved me enough to be the bad guy when a bad guy was what I needed. And on that day it was exactly what I needed.

> My mom loved me enough to be the bad guy when a bad guy was what I needed.

After yet another surgery to deal with the scar tissue, I eventually made it back to school in a wheelchair. I had missed almost half of the year, and even then was nowhere near fully recovered.

Oh, pain, I know thee well.

And I'm not really fond of you.

Pain has helped shape who I am, which is why I wanted to devote a chapter to it. I know that many of the people who pick up this book will be going through their own miseries. If you are, my heart goes out to you. Let me share a few conclusions I've come to.

First, pain offers you as much as it takes from you, and sometimes more.

About a year after I lost my hearing—this was before my music career took off—Dad and I were riding in the car together and talking about what I had been through and was going through. The primary focus of that conversation was how I had become a better person. I was more sensitive to other people's pain. I was more appreciative of little blessings. I had a better sense of what was truly important. And, perhaps most important of all, I had lost a lot of my fear. Things that once intimidated me no longer did. I figured that no failure could possibly be worse than what I had been through, so why not go for it?

Would I have made those improvements in myself without the pain I suffered? Maybe, but I doubt it. Before the trauma, I was mostly just interested in me. I didn't mistreat people or anything like that. I just didn't think very far beyond my own interests. Now everyone says I am a different person, and by different, they mean better.

Which is why, if I were given a chance to do it all again without the trauma, I would decline. That might sound crazy, but I've given it a lot of thought and I truly believe that what I've gotten from my painful experiences is more precious than what I lost. If you assess your situation honestly, you may come to the same conclusion.

> If I were given a chance to do it all again without the trauma, I would decline.

Second, when you're experiencing intense pain, it's important to listen.

Imagine yourself in a deep hole. You can spin around in every direction—north, south, east, or west—and all you'll see is dirt. You can even yell and scream, which is not a bad idea. But you probably won't get out until you listen to someone who is outside the hole.

But that's not always easy to do. There is a tendency to believe that people who are outside the hole can never understand what it's like to be in a hole. Yet the truth is that a lot of people who are outside the hole were once inside the hole, and even if they weren't, or if maybe they were in a different hole, they're now outside the hole, which is where you want to be. So whatever you do, don't write them off. It would be like someone who was starving ignoring the person who has food. Or thinking, "Because he's not hungry, he can't help me."

There is a tendency to believe that people who are outside the hole can never understand what it's like to be in a hole.

Is there someone close to you right now that you need to be listening to? Someone who might be able to speak truth into your situation? Be a voice of reason among all the negative voices in your head? Maybe even spark an idea that could turn your situation, or at least your thinking, in a different direction?

Cynthia Vaughn, my voice teacher, whom I talked about previously in this book, is a person who was outside the hole I was trapped in. I could have concluded that she didn't understand what I was going through and written off her advice to try singing in public at Jay's Bistro. I'm glad I didn't. My being willing to listen to someone who was outside the hole was a game changer.

Third, it's important to live a story, not just a tragedy.

Girl music major goes deaf is a tragedy.

Girl music major goes deaf and then starts to sing again is a story.

In other words, if you allow your pain to define you . . . if you decide to live in it and let it be who you are, that's a tragedy. But if you see your tragic experience as only one mark on the timeline of your life and determine to move past it and make more marks, that's a story.

You probably know people who fit both of these scenarios.

You may have a coworker who hauls her tragedy around with her like Santa hauls his sack of gifts. Everywhere she goes, the sack goes. Every conversation, in some way, has to lead back to what's in the sack. Every failure is because of what's in the sack. Every new friend or acquaintance has to hear about what's in the sack. That crazy sack becomes the person's identity.

But you also surely know people who have suffered terribly, only to go on and be known for something far more significant than their tragedy. That's the kind of person I have made up my mind to be. I say "made up my mind" because moving past a tragic event is not easy. It's much easier just to turn your life into one big pity party and let your tragedy be your excuse for not doing anything.

Looking back, I can point to numerous moments when I faced down my fears and took steps that some would have said were unthinkable. But those moments are the reason I am not living a tragedy today. I won't say that I have completely moved past my tragedy. With a thing like deafness, it's always going to affect you. But it doesn't define me. I don't carry it around in a sack and shove it in the face of everyone I meet.

As I wrap up this chapter, let me share a powerful Scripture verse. Psalm 81:16 (NLT) says, "But I would feed you with the finest wheat. I would satisfy you with wild honey from the rock."

Whoever heard of honey coming from a rock?

Honey is one of the sweetest things found in nature, while a rock is one of the coldest, hardest, and least inviting. Honey and biscuits go together, or honey and hush puppies, but not honey and rocks.

Or do they?

I think the verse means that sweetness can come from the hardest things. That cold, hard rock that you'd never choose to pick up and carry can produce some of life's sweetest blessings. It's certainly been true in my life. It's why I think of pain as a friend masquerading as a monster.

My prayer is that you'll find honey in your rock, too.

making sense of YOUR *rhythm*

Making friends with pain:

+ Pain offers you as much as it takes from you, and sometimes more.

+ When you're experiencing intense pain, it's important to listen.

+ Rather than living a tragedy, live a story.

Closing Encouragement

would feed you with the finest wheat. I would satisfy you with wild honey from the rock.

—Psalms 81:16 (NLT)

My prayer is that you'll find honey in your rock, too.

It's a mistake to confuse pity with love.[13]

—Stanley Kubrick

thirteen

pity is a monster
masquerading as a friend

I understand that most people don't know what to say when they encounter a person with a disability. Maybe it's because they don't encounter disabled people very often. Or perhaps they're concerned about saying the wrong thing or something politically incorrect. (Who can keep up with what's acceptable or unacceptable at any given moment?) Or it could be uncertainty regarding the disabled person's circumstances and outlook. You might expect that long-disabled people would be in a different place emotionally than those who have been disabled only recently. But who knows?

So I get it, I do. And I have no interest in taking shots at people who have been, shall we say, inelegant in the way they have interacted with disabled people. We've all been inelegant at one time or another. But there is one thing you should not say to a disabled person, and that's any form of "Oh, I feel so sorry for you!"

Most disabled people have said it at one time or another: "I don't want your pity!" Sometimes it's said calmly, sometimes through tears, other times in an explosion of anger. Some non-disabled people have told me that they're uncertain what I mean by "pity." What's the difference between *sympathy, empathy,* and *pity*? So I'd like to try to make sense of this, and I want to start with a story.

When I was in college at Colorado State University, I sang in the concert choir as I gradually lost my hearing. There came a day during the second semester that we had an adjunct professor whose job it was to teach us a difficult piece of music that was about twenty minutes long. He chose to have us listen to a recording done by another choir. This wasn't going to work for me the way it was for the other students, so I asked for permission to go to one of the practice rooms with the sheet music and use the piano to try to find my notes and work through the arrangement in my own way. (Keep in mind, at this time my college career was sinking fast, though I was trying as hard as I could to hang on by my fingernails. It would prove to be a futile effort, but at least I hadn't given up yet at that point.)

He wouldn't let me.

He understood that I had lost much of my hearing and couldn't hear the recording well enough to learn from it, but it didn't matter. He made a judgment call for reasons only he could explain. The problem was, it set me up to have pity rained down on me from the other students. They sensed my frustration, which is not a bad thing, but then they started trying to rescue me. They pleaded my case. One or two offered to accompany me to the practice room, which made me feel like a five-year-old. I hate being the center of attention, and suddenly I was. My friends were determined to make the teacher see the error of his way, and he was determined not to change his mind. They actually argued about whether I should be allowed to go practice on my own, which made me feel like I was a problem, that everyone would be better off if I just wasn't there.

And here we get to the heart of why pity is a monster. It turns you into a problem. You're the broken person who needs to be fixed, the problem person who disrupts things for others, the helpless person who needs to be rescued.

> Pity turns you into a problem. You're the broken person who needs to be fixed, the helpless person who needs to be rescued.

Sympathy says, *"I'm sorry for your situation."*

That's fine.

Empathy says, *"I care about your situation."*

That's fine, too.

Pity says, *"You poor thing. What are we going to do with you?"*

That's not fine.

Being deaf does not make me a damsel in distress. I have a disability or, if you prefer, a challenge that I face every day. But who doesn't? You, as you hold this book in your hands, have a challenge of some sort (or maybe several) that you deal with. It could be physical or not. It doesn't mean you're broken, it simply means you're human. It doesn't mean you need to be rescued or fixed, it simply means you have some work to do in learning how to meet the challenge in front of you.

Welcome to the real world.

With that said, let me offer you some dos and don'ts for interacting with disabled people. Keep in mind, you might find some people who would disagree with some of this list, but if you follow it as a general rule, you'll never go too far wrong.

Let's start with the don'ts.

First, don't try to rescue disabled people.

I get that it's a natural impulse for people who care. My dad, for example, has shared his own struggle with this—like when our family goes into a restaurant. The server has no idea I'm deaf and may or may not speak directly to me in a way that enables me to read her lips. Dad's loving impulse is to be proactive and try to avoid an awkward moment by saying, "My daughter is deaf, so you'll need to look at her when you speak, and enunciate." But if he did that, he would be rescuing me and, by implication, suggesting that I am not capable of handling the situation myself, when in fact, I am perfectly capable.

I'll say it again: I am not a damsel in distress.

If I can't understand the server, I can speak for myself and get the problem corrected. I'll say it again: I am not a damsel in distress.

The thing to remember is that "disability" doesn't mean "no ability." When you encounter disabled people, simply use common sense and be polite. If you see someone struggling, step up and lend a hand like you would with anyone else. But allow people to do things for themselves when they can, which will be most of the time.

Second, don't ever say, "I know exactly how you feel."

I am amazed at the number of hearing people who say this to me.

What they mean is that they lost something they treasured, too, so we are alike. No, we aren't. Losing your hearing is not like losing your career or your husband or your house or whatever. Every life challenge is unique and requires different adjustments. In addition, no two people have exactly the same dreams, personality, upbringing, worldview, pain tolerance, support system, or faith, which means they could have exactly the same experience and not process it or react to it in the same way.

When you tell me you know exactly how I feel, you reduce me to the size of *your* experience and understanding, which may not even be close to my reality. And I know that, which makes your words sound incredibly hollow and meaningless to my ears. And yes, irritating. It's always best just to admit that you can't ever know exactly how someone else feels. You can love them and pray for them and even help them if they need it, which they will likely appreciate. But don't suggest that you know exactly how they feel.

Third, don't assume that disabled people are unhappy.

It's easy for someone who can hear to think about my situation and imagine what it must be like not being able to listen to their favorite music or hear their loved ones' voices. The sadness of that thought touches them and they think what an awful life that would be. From there it's a very small step to concluding that I must be miserable. But I'm not, and one reason is that I've had some time to adjust to being deaf. I've learned sign language, learned to read lips, learned how to overcome many of the challenges deaf people face. I've even learned how to sing again. And through that process, and with God's blessings, I've built a very nice life for myself.

Try going to a wheelchair basketball game sometime. Those are some incredible athletes, let me tell you. And they love what they do. They have as much passion for their game as any college or NBA player, and maybe more. And after the game you'll see them with their wives and kids, heading away from the gym laughing and high-fiving.

My own life experiences and my work with disabled people have taught me that disabled people are just like everyone else when it comes to happiness. They can be happy or not happy, but even when they are unhappy, it often has nothing to do with their disability.

> Disabled people have taught me that disabled people are just like everyone else when it comes to happiness.

Fourth, don't decide for disabled people what they need or want.

I've been with a group of friends when they impulsively decided to go to the movies, then one of them froze and said, "Oh, but Mandy's with us. She wouldn't want to do that. We'll think of something else to do." And with that statement I once again become the problem person who disrupts things for others.

It would be much better to go ahead and go to the movies and let me decide if I want to go. If you do it that way, you accomplish two very important things. One, you don't leave me with the awful feeling that I have ruined everyone's evening. And two, you allow me the courtesy of making my own decision instead of, again, rescuing me from what you think is an awkward moment but really isn't. You see, I can actually enjoy a lot of movies, even without hearing. The visuals are so incredible these days; movies are a feast for the eyes, with or without the ears being involved. And there's also just the joy of being with friends. That is meaningful to me no matter what we're doing.

There's an old saying about what happens when you assume. Not making assumptions is at the heart of this suggestion. Don't assume you know what a disabled person would want to do.

Fifth, don't lower standards or expectations to accommodate disabled people.

We live in a culture that gives trophies to losers so no one will feel bad. Somewhere in that twisted psychology is the notion that people are so fragile they can't handle any kind of disappointment. Hence, the common practice of lowering expectations and winking at the failures of people who are disadvantaged in some way.

Believe me when I tell you, we disabled folks want to earn what we got. In fact, a lot of our joy in life comes when we clear hurdles, when we accomplish things in spite of our challenges. If you lower expectations and give us what we haven't earned, then we feel pitied and, even worse, are robbed of the joy of accomplishment.

Plus, it just isn't fair. If an employer gives me a job simply because she feels sorry for me, the applicant who is better qualified has every right to be angry. If a teacher gives me a passing grade I didn't earn simply because she feels sorry for me, the student who worked like crazy to make that same grade has every right to be angry. And ultimately, that anger is going to be directed at me. Not the teacher, not the employer, but me, the one who is reaping the benefits of an unfair system.

You don't need to be afraid of crushing the spirit of a disabled person by expecting him or her to measure up to established standards.

> We disabled people know better than anyone that life isn't fair. We're prepared to do our best and sink or swim like everyone else.

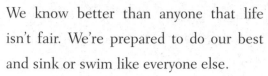

We know better than anyone that life isn't fair. We're prepared to do our best and sink or swim like everyone else.

Finally, don't tell disabled people that you're going to pray for God to take away their disability.

Please don't misunderstand . . . I believe in the power of prayer. Or rather, the power of God to perform miracles, often because we pray. But put yourself in my shoes for a moment. I started going deaf as a freshman in college more than ten years ago. Don't you think I prayed during my descent into silence? Don't you think my family prayed? And my friends? Some of us prayed until our throats were raw. We prayed every kind of prayer we could think of to pray. We prayed until we were prayed out. And yes, we still pray. The problem with telling a disabled person you're going to pray for God to take away their disability is that, whether you mean to or not, you're implying that you believe God will respond to your prayers in a way that he hasn't responded to the thousands of prayers that have already gone up.

What you should do is just pray. You don't have to say you're praying, just pray. And you can pray for some kind of miraculous reversal of the person's disability if you want, but chances are, the disabled person has many other, more pressing needs. We need patience, strength, wisdom, encouragement, and many other things because guess what . . . we're just like you!

So now that you've considered these don'ts, let me suggest a few dos for your interactions with disabled people. And, as you'll note, some of these dos have companion don'ts.

First, do ask about the person's disability if you're curious.

I don't mind when people question me, as long as the questions don't become inappropriately personal and as long as the moment is right. I realize people struggle with life, and sometimes a conversation with someone who's been deep in darkness can be helpful. Or maybe you're losing your hearing or know someone who is. I am happy to share what I've experienced and learned.

However, don't expect me to have all the answers to your problems, to become your personal counselor, or to take you under my wing to raise. A conversation is one thing, but I am not a counselor. I am not qualified to shepherd you through the minefield of your life. Please don't interpret my accessibility and friendliness as an offer to be your go-to person whenever you have a bad day. I hope that doesn't sound cold. I don't mean for it to be. I've just learned that some people can be inappropriately pushy and presumptuous. Speaking for disabled people everywhere, I invite you to ask any questions you might have, but don't expect more from us than is reasonable.

Second, do be thoughtful of a person's disability without being solicitous.

People with disabilities appreciate thoughtfulness just like anyone else. But there's a difference between kind concern and unwelcomed smothering. I'm sure you've heard the term "helicopter parents." These parents hover around their kids 24/7, watching over them, making sure they have what they need, ensuring that no one mistreats them, etc. They are not just concerned about their kids, they are anxious about them to the point of never being able to relax. People who have a solicitous parent or spouse often talk about feeling smothered.

Disabled people don't want to be smothered. We don't want people hovering around us, doing things for us that we can do for ourselves. We don't like to be treated like we might break into pieces at any moment. We simply want the people we meet to be thoughtful. For example, if you see someone in a wheelchair struggling to reach an item on a grocery store shelf, step up and grab that item with a smile and a friendly greeting. But don't follow the person around the store and start grabbing all their items for them.

Third, do use identity-first language.

For example, instead of saying, "She's his blind sister," just say, "She's his sister." Then if it's necessary to the point you're making, you might add that she happens to be blind. But let her just be his sister first and foremost.

The problem with disability-first language is that it traps the disabled person in a stereotype and cultivates pity in other people. For example, when you hear "She's his blind sister," you automatically feel sorry for the sister and assume that she lives a restricted, difficult, and perhaps even unhappy life, when the opposite may be the case. Countless blind people live joyous lives of significant accomplishment. Their disability is far from the most important aspect of their personhood, so what sense does it make to attach the word to their names?

You wouldn't say "She's his uneducated sister" or "divorced sister" or "financially strapped sister" because, while such facts may be true, you wouldn't want to elevate them to a greater level of significance than they deserve. You understand that there are many facts about a person that are more important than her education level, marital status, or bank balance. The same goes for disabled people. In my view, all people deserve the opportunity to demonstrate what kind of people they are without having to first fight through a label or a stereotype.

Finally, keep in mind that some disabilities are invisible.

There's a *Seinfeld* episode where Jerry grows frustrated with an airline employee because she seemed to be ignoring him. Finally, he blurts out in anger, "Are you deaf?" And of course, she was, which caused Jerry untold shame and embarrassment.

You know what the best rule of thumb is? Just be nice to everybody. Be patient with everybody. Invisible disabilities are all around you. And keep in mind that some people's disabilities vary in severity from day to day. A person with arthritis, for example, can feel pretty good one day and be almost unable to get out of a chair the next. Instead of harshly judging people you don't know, just assume that everyone you meet is dealing with something you can't see and be ready to cut some slack. And this kind of assumption doesn't portray you or anyone else as . . . a donkey.

> You know what the best rule of thumb is? Just be nice to everybody. Be patient with everybody.

I'd like to tell you about RC Robinson. At the age of six, he started losing his eyesight. It was the 1930s, and the local doctor had no answers, other than prescribing some ointment and eye drops. He told RC's mother, Retha, that the poor boy would soon be completely blind.

Naturally, everyone who knew the family was heartbroken. Everyone wanted to coddle the boy, but his mother wouldn't stand for it. She put him to work and even made him scrub the floors. People gossiped about how hard she was on him, but she was determined that he would not be pitied, for there would come a time when she wouldn't be around to watch out for him and he would need to be able to stand on his own two feet.

When RC was seven years old, she put him on a train and sent him to St. Augustine, Florida, so he could attend the Florida School for the Deaf and Blind. She gave him a kiss and told him to mind his teachers, then stood back and watched the train chug away into the distance.

Within one year, RC was showing an aptitude for music and was taking piano lessons, while learning to read music in Braille. He also sang in the chorus and huddled around the radio at night to listen to jazz musicians. It would be the beginning of a life in music that turned out to be so extraordinary his nickname became "The Genius."

Yes, I'm talking about Ray Charles Robinson, known to the world as Ray Charles.

Charles recorded at least sixty-four albums, not counting the countless tributes and compilations that are still being released years after his death.

He was given a star on the Hollywood Walk of Fame.

He was inducted into the Rock and Roll Hall of Fame at its inaugural ceremony in 1986.

He was awarded the Grammy Award for Lifetime Achievement.

He had a stamp issued in his honor by the United States Postal Service.

And these honors only scratch the surface of his accomplishments, all because his mother refused to let him be pitied.

She could have rescued him. She could have kept him home and protected him from the mean old world. She could have made life easy for him. Instead, she pushed him to learn to do things for himself and not complain. I have no doubt she shed many a tear along the way, especially the day she put him on that train. But by doing so, she not only saved his life, she gave him a life he never would have had otherwise. And the world is eternally grateful.

> She could have rescued him. Instead, she pushed him to learn to do things for himself and not complain.

Disabled people need a lot of things. The one thing we don't need is pity.

making sense of
YOUR *rhythm*

Dos and don'ts for being kind, rather than expressing pity:

+ *Don't* try to rescue someone with a disability; simply extend common courtesy.

+ *Don't* say, "I know just how you feel"—none of us knows exactly how anyone else feels.

+ *Don't* assume that disabled people are unhappy— they can know the same joy and love of life that you do.

+ *Don't* try to decide what a disabled person needs or wants—they can make their own decisions, just like you.

+ *Don't* lower standards or expectations because someone is disabled—allow everyone to compete or perform on a level playing field.

+ *Don't* say you'll pray that God will take away their disability; just pray.

* *Do* ask about a person's disability if you're curious, being mindful not to pry.

* *Do* be thoughtful about their special needs without hovering or smothering.

* *Do* use "identity-first" language, rather than "disability-first" descriptions.

* *Do* remember that some disabilities are invisible.

Closing Encouragement

Remember that "disability" does not mean "no ability." Be polite and offer to help if appropriate, but allow people to do for themselves when they can—which is most of the time.

Fear is a thief.[14]

—Neil T. Anderson

fourteen

fear will take as much from you as you allow

*I*n *The Wizard of Oz*, the lion is a great big coward. He hides it, at least at first, with a lot of bluster. But when you're a "dandelion," as he confesses in his song, it's going to come out sooner or later. Bluster and big talk only work until Dorothy—or life—calls your bluff. I know about this because I, too, am something of a dandelion.

I've always had a lot of fears. Among them are:

The fear of heights. A lot of people are intimidated by mountains or tall buildings. I'm not all that crazy about stepladders.

The fear of the dark. Many people grow out of this long before they become adults. Not me. This particular fear has gotten worse since I lost my hearing. So much of our sense of safety in the dark comes from being able to hear what's happening around us. Without that, dark places become even more frightening.

The fear of water. Maybe this is more what you'd call an overactive imagination, but when I'm wading in the ocean, I always picture a predator under the surface, circling and sizing me up.

The fear of public presentations. This one I share with about 98 percent of the population.

The fear of injury. This stems from my connective tissue disorder, which causes my joints to dislocate and my bones to break. A fall that most people would jump right up from could seriously hurt me, like the fall I took in PE that I shared earlier.

And since I lost my hearing, a couple of new fears have cropped up: one is the fear of losing my sight. Perhaps this is normal for people who lose one of their primary senses, I don't know. I just know that my eyesight isn't good, and if I were to lose it in addition to my hearing, my life would get infinitely more difficult. I think about it a lot.

> Since I lost my hearing, the fear of losing my sight has cropped up.

The other fear I've had to start dealing with is what I call simply the fear of danger. Because I can't hear, I feel vulnerable to so many more threats. There's always the feeling that things are happening around me that I'm not aware of, things that could hurt me.

As I reflect on my fears, I realize that some of them are a bit hypothetical. For example, the likelihood of there being a snake or a frog in my toilet bowl or a shark in a swimming pool is minuscule. However, other fears are very real and constantly being reinforced by experiences.

For example, on my first date with Travis, we walked down the 16th Street Mall in Denver. It was nighttime, and there was a lot going on. I could feel vibrations from a variety of sound sources, everything from music to car engines. Suddenly, Travis grabbed my arm and roughly jerked me backward. It turned out that we were walking past the entrance to an alley from which a car was emerging. The driver had honked, but with all the other vibrations bombarding my body, I hadn't felt it. The driver, assuming I could hear and would stop, only stomped on the brake at the very last instant. I was literally a split second from being hit by a car.

And then there was the time I moved into my first apartment. I explained to my landlord that I was deaf and needed a fire alarm that flashed. He assured me that a flashing one had been installed and I had nothing to worry about. I checked it out and thought it looked like a normal non-flashing alarm, but I'd never actually seen a flashing one made for a residence, so I took his word for it.

A couple of weeks later, my neighbors had a small fire on their stove while cooking. Across the hall, I was in bed asleep. Sure enough, alarms started screeching, including my own, which I couldn't hear. People were scurrying to get out of the building while I slept blissfully on. It was only when my service dog, Annie, climbed on top of me, as she was trained to do, that I woke up and realized something was happening. The fire wasn't serious, but what if it had been, and what if I hadn't had Annie?

Earlier in the book, I wrote about the time I got run over from behind by a bicyclist who called out to let me know he was coming. He assumed I could hear and would step to the side, which I couldn't and didn't, resulting in a pileup. Since then I've even been paranoid about going for a walk.

It's bad enough to have a fear, it's even worse to have that fear reinforced by a bad experience. From that point on, every time the fear emerges, your brain rewinds to that moment when it proved to be more than just hypothetical, and it screams at you, "Remember, it really *did* happen. And if it happened once it could happen again."

Of course, some fear is a good thing. It's fear that causes us to lock our doors, wear our seat belts, drive the speed limit (or at least close to it), stay away from bad neighborhoods, and say no to that second cheeseburger. But debilitating fear is not a good thing. It will steal good things from you, and it causes you to miss out on so many of the wonderful things life has to offer. I've missed out on several good things, or at least failed to enjoy them, because some inner fear was screaming at me to beware of disaster.

So let me tell you how I made progress with my fear. I won't say I've conquered them all, but I'm not quite the scaredy cat I used to be, and I hope to continue making progress in the future. Perhaps some of these steps I took will help you.

The first thing I did was to accept that I don't have to completely eliminate a fear, I only have to be its boss.

I don't have to completely eliminate a fear, I only have to be its boss.

I finally realized that when I was asking, "How can I get rid of these fears?" I was asking the wrong question. The right question is, "How can I take control of these fears?" That's an important distinction, because the first question had me trying to do the impossible. No amount of praying or reading or counseling or talking to myself was going to make my fears suddenly vanish. If anything, it all made me feel like a failure because, no matter how hard I tried to get rid of them, my fears were always right there, licking their chops, waiting to pounce.

The problem, of course, is that we are made of dust. We are weak, fragile, fallible people and that weakness isn't just in our bodies, it's also in our minds. In fact, I suspect that most people's biggest problems are between their ears. Every now and then I'll encounter a muscular, superhero kind of guy who is terrified of spiders or mice or some other tiny creature that he has complete superiority over. It's entirely a mental thing. Call it the "creep factor." We all deal with it, which, in a way, is encouraging.

Second, I learned to appreciate the value of preparation.

How do you explain the fact that people who do some of the most dangerous jobs are some of the most courageous people? Like Special Forces soldiers, for example. They go into hot spots where danger is multiplied ten times over, but they don't panic; and the vast majority of the time they accomplish their mission. The answer is preparation and training. They understand that because of the risks they're taking, they must keep their skills honed to a razor's edge. They may only do an occasional mission, but they train every day.

And what works for them will work for you and me. You may not be storming enemy strongholds, but if you have a difficult job to do—anything from a test at school to a job interview to a presentation before a prospective client—you can dial down your fear by making sure you're fully prepared. There's no greater feeling than walking into a meeting or a test with the assurance that you know the material forward and backward.

What this means is that being the boss of some fears involves plain old hard work. There's no amount of mental gymnastics that can help you if you aren't prepared.

Third, I've come to realize the importance of surrounding myself with the right people.

Back when I was singing at Jay's Bistro, some people from a group called No Barriers USA heard me and invited me to sing at a planning session for one of their events. I sang one song, a capella, and received an orchid for payment. If that sounds like a raw deal, think again. I actually came out way ahead because that was the event that connected me with No Barriers USA, which has had a profound influence on my life.

The stated purpose of No Barriers USA is to release the potential of the human spirit. One of the founders, Erik Weihenmayer, became the first blind person to climb Mount Everest on May 25, 2001. At the age of thirty-three, he became one of fewer than one hundred people in the world who had climbed the Seven Summits, which are the highest peaks on each of the seven continents. That's the kind of spirit that drives No Barriers USA. They are determined to help people to reach their highest potential. "What's within you is stronger than what's in your way" is one of their favorite sayings.

Just this past year I was at the No Barriers USA summit in Copper Mountain, Colorado. I was scheduled to speak but was taking a break on a picnic bench that just happened to be near a rock-climbing wall. Near me sat a woman, a conference attendee. She struck up a conversation with me, pointing out how she had a fear of heights and would never be able to climb that wall. I told her I was afraid of heights, too. Before we knew it, we had talked ourselves into one of those middle-school pacts kids make: "I'll do it if you'll do it." Suddenly, we were being strapped into our harnesses, and I'm not sure how, but I had been designated to go first.

Understand, this was really scary for me. That rock wall was two stories high! But there's something about being in an environment where people are being encouraged and challenged to break through barriers. I made up my mind I was going up that thing. I was determined. I was confident. I was seeing visions of future glory . . .

Okay, let's be honest . . . I was terrified.

My heart felt like a tennis ball repeatedly whacking against my chest wall. My breathing was shallow. My mind was racing, trying to think of excuses that would get me out of this ridiculous pact I had made. How could I have been so stupid?

I decided that I would go up a little ways and then make up some reason to have to go down; but when that moment came, a strange thing happened. Down below me the woman with whom I'd made the pact was clapping and cheering. I could see her shake her fist in the air and urge me on. Then I looked to my right and saw another climber. A lump the size of a grapefruit came into my throat when I saw that he had one functioning limb. He was strapped into his harness and was using his leg to push himself up inches at a time.

That day I went up and down that wall three times. And I can tell you the exact moment when I went from being my fear's slave to being its boss. It was when I saw the people around me cheering and challenging me not to give up.

Back at the very beginning of time, God said that it isn't good for people to be alone. There are probably lots of reasons why this is true, but one of them surely is that when we meet seemingly insurmountable challenges, we need someone beside us to scream, "You can do it!"

If you have a fear that gives you trouble, surround yourself with people who won't let you surrender to it. It might be someone who has conquered that same fear, or maybe not. At the very least, it must be someone who loves you enough to want to push you to be the very best you can be.

The fourth thing I've learned is that overcoming fear, like any challenge, is a process.

You don't do it in a day, sometimes not in a month, a year, or even a lifetime. The point is that you keep chipping away at it. You never, ever declare the battle lost, even if you have a bad moment. You just regroup and try again.

> Never, ever declare the battle lost, even if you have a bad moment. Just regroup and try again.

I have no credentials in the world of psychology, but I do know that when it comes to fears and phobias, almost everyone agrees that some kind of exposure therapy helps. In other words, you expose yourself to the thing you're afraid of. Ideally, you'll discover that the monster wasn't a monster at all. Or at least, that its bark was worse than its bite.

The time I experienced exposure therapy in a life-changing way was the first time I sang at Jay's Bistro. I had imagined every disaster scenario my little brain could conjure up. Still, I found a way to push through, and not only lived to tell about it, but actually had a positive experience that led to more and more opportunities to sing.

I'm telling you right now that you'll never be the boss of your fear if you keep running from it. You must stand up to it. Let it throw its best punch. Even if it wins the first round, you can come out for the second round a little wiser and a little better prepared. Many boxers lose the early rounds of the fight only to come back to win. The key is to take the long view and not be discouraged by a bad experience.

You'll never be the boss of your fear if you keep running from it.

It's been written that the Bible says not to be afraid over three hundred times, but then mentions at least two hundred people who were afraid. Isn't that interesting? What if the Bible said three hundred times not to cheat on your taxes, and then turned around and told two hundred stories about people who cheated on their taxes? Wouldn't it be better to tell stories about people who *didn't* cheat on their taxes? Wouldn't it be better to tell stories about people who *weren't* afraid?

Ah, but here's the difference: Being afraid is nothing like cheating on your taxes. Cheating on taxes is a calculated maneuver while fear is an emotional response. If, somehow, we could take emotion out of the picture, we could think through every situation logically and eliminate most or all of our fear. But if we took emotion out of the picture, we might lose our fear, but we would also lose love and hope and encouragement and joy and so many of the other emotions that make life so wonderful.

And this is life: The good is so often commingled with the bad.

Poison ivy sprouts up among the wild flowers.

Bad employees clock in alongside the good ones.

Wolves creep in among the sheep.

Fear sleeps in the same bunk bed with love.

The difference is in how many places you set at the table. You can treat fear like it belongs or like an outsider. You can accept what it takes from you or decide you've lost enough. You can let it take you hostage or show it who's boss.

May God help us to choose wisely the next time the thief comes sauntering through the door.

making sense of
YOUR *rhythm*

How to become the boss of your pain:

+ Remember that you don't have to completely eliminate fear in order to be its boss.

+ You can dial back your fear by making sure you're fully prepared.

+ Surround yourself with people who will cheer you on and challenge you to try.

+ Overcoming fear is a process. If you have a bad moment, regroup and try again.

Closing Encouragement

You can let fear take you hostage, or you can show it who's boss. May God help us to choose wisely the next time this thief tries to steal our joy.

Sometimes it's not good enough to do your best; you have to do what's required.[15]

—Winston Churchill

fifteen

there really is a recipe for success

ooks on how to be successful are a dime a dozen. Take them out of your local bookstore and the shelves would be half-empty. For that reason, it's easy not to take them seriously, to regard them as fluff, or perhaps as just another way for someone life has smiled on to make a buck. Because, truly, some people do seem to almost stumble into success. I'm sure you know people, as I do, who were born into money or blessed with a family name that opened doors or who married the CEO's daughter or who was just standing in the right spot at the right moment. People like that can quickly turn you into a cynic when you've worked your fingers to the bone and seen none of your dreams come true.

I think we have to admit that there's no rational explanation for some people's success, or lack thereof. Pick any profession, and you'll find people who will make you scratch your head with wonder at how they made it to the top, and other people who seem obviously more gifted than their bosses but are languishing at the bottom of the food chain. I offer no theories on this. Sometimes life just makes no sense.

I believe that, for most people, there is a rhyme and reason to this thing we call success.

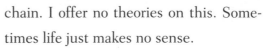

However, I do believe that, for most people, there is a rhyme and reason to this thing we call success. For every one person who stumbles into it, there are probably a thousand—maybe a million—who thoughtfully, systematically chase it down. In this chapter, I want to talk about what I've learned about success on my own journey.

Of course, different people define success in different ways. For some, it's all about money and the things money can buy. If you have the big house, the fancy car, and the ritzy address, you're successful. It doesn't matter if you're on your fourth marriage and your kids won't speak to you, you've got the trappings of success and that's all that matters.

For others, success is only about the dream. These people set out in pursuit of a specific dream and can never be satisfied until it's in their hands. They may become so desperate to achieve their dream that they resort to all sorts of questionable behaviors that bring heartache into their lives. And if they don't achieve exactly what they envisioned, they feel like they failed.

For other people, success is more about being happy. We all know someone who lives paycheck to paycheck in a house with a leaky roof, but always seems to be of good cheer. He enjoys his hourly wage job, his marriage brings him joy, and his kids climb all over him and smother him in kisses. Ask him if he feels successful and he'll say yes.

Everyone has to define success in their own way, but it seems to me that without happiness, the rest of it doesn't matter much. I'm not dissing riches or the pursuit of dreams. I'm just saying that if you're not happy, it's all going to seem hollow and unsatisfying.

I began to think about what success might look like for me when I was a singer back in 2011. That was the year I won the VSA International Young Soloist Competition. It's a scholarship program for musicians under the age of twenty-five who have some sort of disability. I was chosen along with James Schlender, a violinist from Montana who was born with aortic stenosis, and Rachel Skleničková, a classical pianist from the Czech Republic, who is blind.

The selection carried a $5,000 prize, which was nice. But the more significant thing for me was the opportunity to perform at the Kennedy Center. Performing at such a legendary venue had long been a dream, and finally I was there. James, Rachel, and I each did a few numbers and then collaborated on "Fly Me to the Moon."

When the concert was over, I had the sickening feeling that it wasn't my talent that got me to the Kennedy Center; it was my disability.

But when the concert was over, I was surprised to find that I did not feel exhilarated. I did not feel like I had planted a flag on top of Mount Everest. Rather, I felt depressed. Why? Because I had the

sickening feeling that it wasn't my talent that got me to the Kennedy Center; it was my disability. It struck me that I never would have been asked to sing there because of my talent alone.

Of course, I wasn't entirely correct in that assessment. The award was an international competition that drew thousands of applicants. The notion that my talent had nothing to do with my winning the award just wasn't true. I beat out some marvelously talented people, and I am extremely grateful to those who chose me. Still, I felt that it was just a onetime thing, that it would never happen again. I assumed I was one and done, and that didn't feel much like success.

Skip ahead one year.

Out of the blue, I received an invitation to perform at the Kennedy Center again, not as an award recipient, but as a vocal artist. I was asked to do a full concert and told that I would not be sharing the stage with other artists. I was allowed to pick my own songs, to do whatever I wanted. In other words, I was treated like a real, honest-to-goodness professional musician. You can imagine how much different that performance felt as compared to the first one. It felt much more like success.

Since then I've been given many more wonderful opportunities. I've been privileged to sing in more legendary venues, to appear on national television shows, to make a commercial, to appear in a documentary called *The Rebound* about a wheelchair basketball team, to record several CDs, and even to write this book for a world-class publisher. I no longer struggle with the idea that people are only interested in me because I am so unusual. I understand that being a deaf singer is interesting, but not interesting enough to sustain a career.

I still have to be able to sing well enough that people want to listen to me. And many do, which feels like success to me.

But this success is not something I stumbled into. I didn't get here by having famous parents or by marrying the record executive's son or by throwing money around. I got here by combining four things that I believe are essential to any person's quest for success. Call them a recipe if you want, that's as good a term as any. I want to talk about each ingredient in case you happen to be on a similar quest. It doesn't matter if you're an aspiring musician or dream of starting your own business. In my experience, these are the things that are baked into success for the majority of us who don't stumble into it.

The first ingredient is passion.

Music has always been my passion. Originally, I wanted to be a choir director. There's just something about pulling together a multitude of voices and producing something beautiful that is appealing to me. But it's impossible to teach and train a choir when you can't hear. I would have no way of knowing when someone was singing off-key or when the voices weren't blending well or when the lyrics were not understandable.

But this is how I know that music is my passion: Even when my original dream evaporated like a puff of smoke, I couldn't let go of music. Yes, I did go through a yearlong period of darkness and depression after I lost my hearing in which I did nothing with music. But when I started to heal emotionally, music was the thing that helped pull me out of the darkness. When Dad and I sat in our basement and sang a little song together, it was as if a tiny ray of sunshine broke through the fog. Suddenly, things didn't seem so hopeless anymore.

Passion is that thing in your gut that keeps you from giving up when a door is slammed in your face.

Which brings me to an important point: Your passion is that thing you can't let go of. Even when circumstances move it out of reach, you just keep trudging after it. Like a writer who sits down day after day and hammers out page after page even though he's been rejected a dozen times. Or like an actress who keeps showing up for casting calls even though she's never received a callback. Passion is that thing in your gut that keeps you from giving up when a door is slammed in your face. It keeps you moving forward when resources and opportunities are limited. In other words, if you can quit and walk away from it for good, it was never your passion.

The second ingredient in success is talent.

Passion without talent will only make you the brunt of jokes. Remember William Hung? He was the Korean-born singer who burst onto the world stage in 2004 because of an off-key rendition of Ricky Martin's song "She Bangs" that he performed on *American Idol*. Simon Cowell made a classic statement: "You can't sing, you can't dance, so what do you want me to say?"

Yes, William Hung's résumé is pretty impressive, considering that he appeared on more than a dozen national TV shows and released three albums. His cult following even demanded that he be brought back to *American Idol*, and so he was . . . on a mid-season special titled *Uncut, Uncensored, and Untalented*. By 2011, the joke had run its course, and William Hung was out of the music business. Only a fool would question William Hung's passion for singing. He probably had enough for twenty people. But passion without talent isn't enough to achieve true success.

One thing you have to understand about talent is that you can have a lot, and it still might not be enough to get you where you want to go. For example, when they do a casting call in New York City or Los Angeles, it's not unusual for hundreds of hopefuls to show up, many of them brimming with talent. Or when you submit your résumé for the job of your dreams, it might land on a stack of résumés from people who are every bit as qualified as you are. Sometimes, factors that have nothing to do with talent determine who gets the job.

Which leads me to say this: Don't be too discouraged when a door slams in your face.

Agatha Christie sent manuscripts to publishers for five years before she got her first book deal. Did that mean she couldn't write? Of course not. She has now sold over two billion books, which is more than any author in history except William Shakespeare. Likewise, Louis L'Amour received over two hundred rejections before he finally got a book deal. Today he is Bantam's all-time bestselling author, with over 300 million books sold. I could go on and on, but you get the idea. A closed door doesn't necessarily mean you have no talent.

So who decides if you're talented enough to make it?

My suggestion is not to listen to your mother. Or the little old ladies at church who love you and will tell you your song was beautiful even if it was terrible. It's much wiser to focus on the opinions of people who are already where you want to be. When one of them says, "You could be where I am," that's significant.

Of course, when all is said and done, the audience will have its say. There's an old saying that the customer is always right. That's silly, of course. Customers are often wrong. However, they do vote with their dollars on everything from restaurants to movies to toothpaste to automobiles. Every employer, manufacturer, publisher, and politician in the world pays attention to what "the people" think. It would be silly for you or me to ignore them.

And the third ingredient to success is plain old hard work.

Passion and talent might enable you to make a splash. But if you're lazy, you'll quickly be surpassed by someone who is just as passionate and talented as you are, but also willing to work hard on his craft. I'm sure you've heard it said that someone was a "flash in the pan." It's a term that comes from the Gold Rush days. It refers to something shiny that grabs the prospector's attention in the pan, but turns out to be nothing of lasting value. That's a perfect description of the talented person who is lazy.

> Passion and talent might enable you to make a splash. But if you're lazy, you'll quickly be surpassed.

Larry Bird is an NBA Hall of Famer who cuts a striking figure at 6 feet 9 inches tall. You see him and immediately you think: basketball player. But other than being tall, Larry Bird did not blow people away with natural ability. He wasn't particularly fast, and he wasn't a great leaper. The thing that made Larry Bird great was his work ethic. He often showed up an hour before his teammates, shooting three hundred shots before any of them made their way onto the court.

As a result, this man of average athletic ability was able to outplay many of his more gifted opponents.

In the business world, Mark Cuban is recognized as extremely successful. Some say he was lucky because he got into technology stocks at exactly the right time. But Cuban is quick to point out that he routinely stayed up studying until 2:00 a.m. to make himself a wise investor and didn't take a vacation the first seven years he was in business.

I could fill the rest of this book with stories about people who achieved extreme success primarily because of their willingness to work harder than everyone else.

In my own case, I have put in countless hours working on my craft, starting with the voice lessons I took from Cynthia Vaughn while I was still in high school. I've learned to sing in different languages to improve my diction and interpretive ability. I've studied different styles of music, everything from jazz to opera. I've picked the brains of other singers and studied the performance techniques of those I haven't had a chance to meet. And I practice. There wouldn't be any way to calculate the amount of time I've spent singing scales and learning songs and rehearsing with my band.

We live in a time when distractions are many. Social media, streaming videos, computer games, and a hundred other things are vying for your time and attention. You need to understand that this is where the battle for success will be won or lost for a lot of people. If you want to excel, you must consistently carve out time to work on your craft.

The fourth and final ingredient in success is opportunity.

You can be passionate, talented, and disciplined, but until you get an opportunity to use your talent in some way that impacts people, it's going to be hard for you to feel successful. And opportunities are tricky. Like I said earlier, sometimes life just makes no sense. The guy doing the hiring might give the job to someone who isn't as talented and hasn't worked nearly as hard as you. You'll whine and complain and wonder what on earth he's thinking. The one thing you won't do is change his mind.

My advice when it comes to opportunities is threefold:

Number one: Be ready at all times because you never know when an opportunity is going to drop into your lap. That means staying on top of your game, even when it seems the whole world has diverted its attention elsewhere. You never know when a door might swing open. The words "I never saw that coming" are spoken every day by people who expected the next day to be exactly like the one before.

Number two: Be humble enough to take the small opportunities. In the movie *La La Land*, Emma Stone's character, Mia Dolan, puts on a one-woman show in a small rented theater. About ten people show up, leaving her so discouraged that she decides to give up on her show business dream. But she later discovers that one of the people who attended was a casting director who was so impressed that she invited Mia to audition for her new movie.

> You do something small and do it well, and suddenly someone is asking you to take on a bigger role.

This kind of thing happens all the time. You do something small and do it well, and suddenly someone is asking you to take on a bigger role.

Number three: Stick to your convictions.

One time I was asked to join a touring band as a backup singer. If you know anything about the music business, you know that a lot of great artists started out as backup singers. Whitney Houston, Mariah Carey, Elton John, Sheryl Crow, and John Legend are just a few examples. The problem was that I knew the members of this band were into heavy drugs and partying. They also wanted me to get breast implants and wear skimpy clothing during the performances. Yes, I would make some money and get myself onto a lot of stages in high-profile venues, but at what price? I decided that nothing I got from them would be worth what I'd have to give up. I urge you not to compromise your values just to get an opportunity. Sooner or later, you'll look back and be sorry you did.

I said earlier in the book that I've learned to break down big challenges and then put the pieces back together in a way that makes sense to me. Well, I broke down this success idea into smaller pieces and then put it back together in a mathematical equation:

Passion + Discipline (but with little or no talent) = A Hobby

Passion + Talent + Opportunity (but with no hard work) = Temporary Success at Best

Passion + Opportunity (but with no talent) = William Hung

Talent + Opportunity (but with no passion) = Drudgery

Passion + Talent + Hard Work + Opportunity = Success

And now, one more thought.

Keep in mind that circumstances have a way of rewriting our definitions. Today, success might look like a music career or a book contract or a corner office or a spouse with 2.4 kids and a dog. It wouldn't take a serious illness long to rewrite any such definition. A simple biopsy could have you defining success as the ability to survive chemo without losing your sense of humor. Or what about a death in the family? In one day your primary goal might go from having a career in music to helping raise your younger siblings.

There's an old saying: Man plans and God laughs.

The point is, life is full of surprises, not all of them good. Trust me, I know. So don't get so committed to one definition of success that you aren't able to adjust. Who knows? Circumstances might force you to redefine success numerous times before all is said and done.

Whatever your definition is at the moment, don't depend on life's quirky twists to get you there. Knuckle down and do what's required.

making sense of YOUR *rhythm*

Four things are baked into success—for the majority of us who don't stumble into it:

- ✦ The first ingredient is passion—that thing you can't let go of.

- ✦ Next is talent—without that, your passion can't take you very far.

- ✦ Third is good ol' hard work—there are lots of talented people in the world, but constant attention to your craft helps you rise above the crowd.

- ✦ Finally, you need opportunity—so when it comes, be ready, be humble, and stick to your convictions.

Closing Encouragement

Whatever your definition of success, don't depend on life's quirky twists to get you there. Knuckle down and do what's required.

*Focus on what you can do
and keep moving forward.*

—my mom

sixteen

caregivers are unsung heroes

The very idea of a love/hate relationship seems absurd. How can you love someone and hate them at the same time? I'm not qualified to explain the psychology of it, but I certainly know the feeling. I love my mom with all my heart, but there were times when the anger I felt toward her was almost otherworldly. You see, she was my primary caregiver during the time I spent recovering from my knee surgeries, and as such it was her job to make me do all the things the doctor told me I must do if I wanted to walk again without a limp. They were hard things, painful things, things no person in their right might would *want* to do.

I told you in an earlier chapter that when the doctor said my leg needed to be bent in order to tear the scar tissue that was building up, Mom was the one who knelt in front of me and did the pushing. To say I didn't appreciate her help in those moments would be putting it mildly.

What I now understand is that my own personal horrors were not the only ones in our home. My goodness, imagine a mother having to inflict such pain on her child. I often think now that those moments were harder for her than they were for me, and they were insanely hard for me.

But it wasn't just Mom. Every member of my family contributed in their own unique ways. Dad, for example, was my encourager. He has a special gift for meaningful conversation. He's a thinker. He has the ability to reason through a situation, to break it down, and to come out on the other end with a sensible perspective or a helpful piece of advice. I'll never forget the times we sat talking and crying together. At the time I was too lost in the fog of my circumstances to appreciate the gift he was giving me.

But my favorite story from those days concerns my younger sister, Sammi, who is a couple of years younger than me. First, you must understand that we didn't get along very well when we were kids. All four of us Harvey kids had different gifts and personalities, creating different levels of compatibility and, ultimately, different levels of connection. I was closer to my older sister, Katie, and Sammi was closer to our younger brother, Josh. Sammi and I didn't hate each other (well, there may have been a few times), but neither were we bosom pals.

When I went off to college, I was thrilled to be out of the house and on my own. No more sharing a room with a sister who mostly just got on my nerves. Sadly, as I have chronicled in earlier chapters, my college career crashed and burned when I lost my hearing. By the time summer came around, I was back home, deaf, emotionally devastated, feeling utterly hopeless, and yes, that's right, ladies and gentlemen, rooming once again with my sister. I felt like a boxer who had been pummeled, who had dropped to the canvas, and had then been kicked in the ribs for good measure. I couldn't imagine life getting any worse.

I was back home, deaf, emotionally devastated, and yes, ladies and gentlemen, rooming once again with my sister.

But then Sammi did something I will never forget.

During the summer before her senior year in high school, she took classes so she would be able to skip her senior year. Her *senior* year! Let that soak in. Your senior year of high school is the one year of school you actually look forward to. It's the one chance—maybe the *only* chance you get in your entire life— to feel like a big shot. After years of being looked down upon by upperclassmen, finally it's *your* chance to strut around and act cocky. Who wants to miss out on *that?* And that's not to mention the perks of being a senior: You get your own prom, most of your classes are easier, and you might get to skip your finals. And don't forget graduation gifts!

Yes, Sammi gave all that up, and do you know why?

She did it for me.

She knew that I would waste away if I just locked myself in our room and never came out, which is exactly what I intended to do. She knew that I needed to do something constructive, like easing back into school by going to Front Range Community College. But she knew I would never do it on my own. It would be my first attempt to reenter the hearing world as a deaf person, which she knew I would find terrifying. The prospect of failure would just seem too great. So she fixed things so she could go with me and help me.

Imagine, Mandy and Sammi, former rivals, taking American Sign Language, literature, history, and English composition together. We were literally a team because Sammi was approved by the college to be my official note taker in class.

Now here's the craziest part of the story.

When Sammi was taking those summer courses before her junior year, I didn't get that she was doing it for me. I'm sure it was talked about in our home, but I was so depressed at the time that I had shut everybody out. It's like I was living in a cave with a boulder rolled in front of the entrance. My parents probably could have turned our living room into a gambling casino and I wouldn't have noticed. Which means that Sammi got no gratitude from me while she was making that sacrifice. Yet she still made it. Happily.

> Sammi got no gratitude from me while she was making that sacrifice. Yet she still made it. Happily.

As I wrap up this book, I want to say a few things to those of you who may be caregivers, or who may fulfill that role someday.

First, you are heroes.

Hero is a word that's thrown around too much today. People are granted hero status simply because they wear a uniform or can sing or can throw a basketball through a hoop with amazing frequency. To my way of thinking, a person who gives care to someone who is hurting, lonely, or in need of help is a *real* hero.

And the caregiving acts I'm talking about don't have to be enormous. Picking up a prescription for an elderly person who can't drive; providing childcare for a baby so his single mom can go to a job interview; dropping off a hot casserole to someone who's recovering from surgery and then staying to visit a while . . . these are things that seem minute in the grand scheme. No medals are given, no articles are written, no fuss is made over the people who do such things. And yet to the people on the receiving end, these small gestures of love and kindness can be life-giving. I'm convinced that some people find the strength to keep going one more day because a small act of kindness from a friend or neighbor has reminded them that someone cares and reassured them that they are loved and have value.

There's no way to measure this statistically. I'm sure policemen and firemen and other emergency responders can tell you exactly how many calls they've gotten and how many people they've saved, but you caregivers often have no idea how much good you're doing. You sense you're doing *some* good, obviously. But it's hard to quantify the value of an act of kindness. I think we would all be shocked to know how many lives have been saved by people who have a heart to help others.

Second, remember that you don't have to meet every need a person has to be effective.

My dad couldn't help me go to school, but he could sit and talk with me when I needed to sort through my emotions and straighten out my thinking. My sister wasn't the right person to help me sort through my emotions and straighten out my thinking, but she could help me go to school. You get the idea. I got different things from different people.

It would have been pointless for my dad to beat himself up because he couldn't help me go to school, or for Sammi to lament her inability to serve as my counselor the way Dad did. But this is often what happens. Caregivers fit into that small group of people who do so much and then feel guilty because they aren't able to do more.

You have to be careful here.

There have been people who actually damaged themselves and/or their families because they weren't able to set healthy boundaries. There are caregivers who crash their finances because they couldn't say no to a friend with money problems. Some endanger themselves by taking homeless people with addictions and criminal records into their homes. Others neglect their own marriages and children because they are so busy trying to help other people with *their* marriages and children.

There are billions of other people in the world. Have a little faith that God will raise up a few of them to do what you can't.

You don't have to meet every need a person has to be effective. Figure out what God has gifted you to do and do it. There are billions of other people in the world. Have a little faith that God will raise up a few of them to do what you can't. And remember, you really aren't accomplishing much if you meet one need in another person's life while creating a new one in your own.

Third, don't get too discouraged when you become the bad guy.

Most people assume that caregiving sets you up for a steady stream of love and appreciation from the person you're helping. But the truth is that caregivers often bear the brunt of a lot of anger and frustration.

I have a friend who was in the hospital with pneumonia. Every day the respiratory therapist would start her shift at 5:00 a.m. by coming to his room and giving him a breathing treatment. On about the fourth morning, he said, "Just once couldn't you do one of your other patients first so I can sleep in?" She responded, "My other three patients yell and curse at me if I wake them up, so I start with you because you're so nice." My friend concluded that nice guys might finish last, but they always get the first breathing treatment of the morning.

Caregiving is not always well received. Sometimes you have to wake people up at 5:00 a.m. Sometimes you have to push them to do physical therapy when they'd rather lie in bed. Sometimes you have to keep them from eating something that will send their blood sugar over the moon. Sometimes you have to bend their knees to rip loose some scar tissue. We often equate "care" with actions that are soft and tender, but care can be brutal, just like love can be tough.

So don't get too discouraged when you become the bad guy. Try to see beyond the anger coming your way. My mom always had the attitude that there were certain things that needed to get done in order for me to get my life back and she was going to see to it that I did them no matter how mad it made me. She didn't focus on the pain of the moment, but on the bigger goal down the road.

Finally, as a caregiver, don't forget to take care of yourself.

One of the big difficulties caregivers face is asking for help in the work of caregiving. Especially if you're caring for a family member, you have a tendency to think, "This is my family member and, therefore, my responsibility." And that's not wrong. But neither is it the end of the matter. Yes, it's your responsibility to care for your family member (or see that he gets cared for), but that doesn't mean you can't ask for some help. Even Jesus, the greatest caregiver of all time, enlisted twelve guys to help him.

You must replenish your spiritual reserves.

Another thing you must do as a caregiver is replenish your spiritual reserves. Here again, we can take a lesson from Jesus, who made it a point to go off by himself and spend time in prayer. Do you ever wonder what he was praying about . . . what he was asking his heavenly Father for in those lonely, quiet moments? Based on his lifestyle, I'm pretty sure he wasn't focused on anything physical. Rather, I suspect his primary concern was on his heart and mind—that he would be able to keep going and not get discouraged or distracted—and on the hearts and minds of those he loved.

During the time that I was losing my hearing, and for several months after that, our home became a difficult place to live. It didn't matter that my mom and dad and all of my siblings are Christians, the catastrophe that was unfolding in my life made their existence infinitely harder. They were heartbroken for me. They had a ringside seat as all my dreams circled the drain and disappeared into the sewage of history. They had to find new ways to interact with me because I suddenly wasn't the same person. They couldn't see the future and didn't know if I would eventually be okay. And worst of all, they had to grapple with some heavy questions about God and his purposes and why so many of our prayers seem to go unanswered. How could any person not grow spiritually weary in a situation like that?

Remember I said earlier that caregivers are heroes? Notice I didn't say *superheroes*. Superheroes are myth and legend. You, dear friend, are not one. So don't act like one. Make sure you take time to refill yourself, or there'll come a day when you won't have anything left to pour into others.

A lot of interesting things are happening in America these days. I'll let you be the judge of whether they're good or bad. One thing I'm sure we can all agree on is that a lot of people care about a lot of things. With all the marching and protesting, one could make the case that people have never cared more. So how is it that with all this caring, there are still so many hurting, anguished people?

The answer is that a lot of the caring we see today is directed toward ideologies, not people. And it's a lot easier to care about an ideology than it is to care for a person. Caring about an ideology

It's a lot easier to care about an ideology than it is to care for a person.

allows you to pick and choose when you want to engage, while caring for a person generally has to be done every single day. Caring for an ideology puts you in the thick of a crowd and makes you instant friends, while caring for a person often isolates you from your friends. Caring for an ideology gets you fired up enough to run through a brick wall, while caring for a person often drains you of what little energy you have left.

The question is often asked, "Who cares?"

Obviously, everybody cares about something. But there's a big difference between caring and giving care.

If you're a caregiver, thank you for your hard work. Somebody's life is a little easier because of you.

making sense of
YOUR *rhythm*

To those of you who are caregivers or someday will be . . .

- ✦ You're nothing short of a hero—your kindness helps another person go on for one more day.

- ✦ You don't have to meet every need of the person you care for to be effective—simply do what God has gifted you to do.

- ✦ Don't get too discouraged when you need to be the bad guy—keep your eye on the bigger goal.

- ✦ Don't forget to take care of yourself—even Jesus stepped away from the crowd to spend time in refreshment.

Closing Encouragement

Dear Caregiver, thank you for your sacrificial service. Someone's life is a little easier because of you.

frequently asked questions

$\mathcal{I}$ decided to devote the final pages of my book to some questions that I seem to get wherever I go. Here they are, in no particular order.

How are you able to sing with such good diction and in tune with your accompaniment? How do you do it?

This is something I work on almost every day. The benefit of losing my hearing as an adult is that I spent eighteen years with sound, hearing and pronouncing words, singing, and speaking clearly. Because I had issues with my hearing as a child, I did a lot of work with Hooked on Phonics, which I'm sure helps my diction to this day. Pitch is a different challenge. I was born with near-perfect pitch, so I can stay in tune throughout a song as long as I get the first note right. I spend part of every day working on my pitch using visual tuners. I find the root note and sing my scales, making sure I hit all the right intervals. I grew up with a love for music theory, so that helps.

Working on scales and intervals is not boring to me like it might be to other people.

How do you write music? Where do you get your inspiration?
I'm inspired by my feelings. I don't overthink that part of it. As for the creation of the melody, I just think it and sing it out loud into a recorder. Then I send the recording to a musician friend who charts it out for me. That way I can see what I've got. "Happy Again" is a song I wrote in one take. I was sitting in my car and hit RECORD on my phone, then sang a song from start to finish off the top of my head. Three and a half minutes later, I ended the recording and never changed a thing. I'm never trying to come up with a hit song, nor do I sing about things I'm not passionate about. I simply focus on how I feel at that moment.

How do vibrations help you sing? How do you adjust to performing in different environments?
Feeling the vibrations from the instruments keeps me in time but also helps me sense dynamic changes in the music. When a room is really loud, there are competing vibrations so I have to rely more on eye contact with the rest of the band. We have a predetermined structure to each song—an arrangement, if you will—but we still communicate visually to get in and out of solos properly and so I will always know when to come back in after a solo. The vibrations that come through the floor help me to feel more connected with what is going on.

Are you aware of the work of Evelyn Glennie, the deaf percussionist, and her documentary Touch the Sound?

I am very much aware of her work and think she is amazing! I have had the honor of meeting her a couple of times. She is simply a brilliant woman.

What advice would you give yourself if you had a time machine and could go back to when you were eighteen and first coming to terms with your hearing loss?

I think I would just leave a note saying "Whatever happens, keep moving forward." I didn't know then what I know now, that all the pain ahead of me would change me for the better. I now appreciate things more and have more empathy for others. It was all a learning experience and a chance to grow. I needed to grieve and to be angry. I needed to cry and to become numb for a time. But I also needed to not give up, to keep moving forward. My biggest temptation was to give up.

When you dream, do you hear sound?

Everyone seems to ask that! The answer is, I don't dream very often, but when I do it's more like a series of snapshots than a movie. I haven't remembered any specific sounds or conversations in my dreams over the past ten years, but I also can't remember any sounds prior to my hearing loss.

How does your connective tissue disorder affect you?

When you have hypermobility, you have to be very cautious, even when you're doing ordinary things. For example, putting on a shirt can cause your shoulder to dislocate. I dislocated my knee while jogging in PE when I was a senior in high school. That horrifying experience taught me to pay attention to what I'm doing and to be careful at all times.

Can you drive?

Yes! Being deaf doesn't make a person an unsafe driver. In fact, I think it makes me a better driver because I am paying more attention and have less to distract me.

Do you play music in the car? Or ever?

Absolutely! I love to feel music. It actually helps me concentrate when I am doing certain tasks. I once got pulled over by a cop because I was playing music too loud in my car. He let me off with a verbal warning about noise ordinances in the community. Sometimes playing music makes me sad because I realize I am missing out on the joy I used to get when listening to it. But I have found enjoyment from playing songs I know very well. An added bonus is that you don't get sick of the same song playing over and over. I once thought I was listening to "Rock the Boat" on a loop. It turned out to be a different song but the beat and structure were the same. It didn't matter. I sang "Rock the Boat" over and over again to myself.

What does music mean to you?

Music is a way of expressing what's in my heart and soul. I want to keep doing it for as long as I possibly can.

If you lost your ability to sing, what would you do?

I do think about that. I made a promise to myself that I would record five albums before I was thirty so I could get a chunk of music laid out in case something happened to my voice. The reason was so I could show my future kids and grandkids that I once had an amazing opportunity and ran with it for as long as I could. I think that if I suddenly couldn't do what I'm doing, I would just think of another way to be involved with music.

Why use ASL (American Sign Language) if you can lip-read?

Lip-reading does not allow for flawless communication. A lip reader only gets pieces of what people say and then tries to figure out what those pieces mean. There are a lot of people who cannot lip-read at all. Even if you are easy to read, I will still get less than 50 percent of what you say. And by the end of the day, I am worn out from the intensity of trying so hard. ASL is a beautiful language that is full of expression. I am continuing to learn and to hopefully improve my skills. Signing while singing brings me joy because, while I sing for others, I sign for me. It's my way to connect to the song and its meaning.

What do you want to do with your career?

I want to do what I am doing now, encouraging others and making people smile. I have a list of albums that I want to make and lots of songs I want to write. I would be perfectly happy making music and doing motivational speaking for the foreseeable future.

What do you love about No Barriers USA?

No Barriers USA is a beautiful organization that has pushed me to reach a potential I didn't know I had. I have seen people achieve what was thought to be impossible because they told themselves that what was within them was stronger than what was in their way. The organization made me realize that the biggest obstacles are the ones created in our minds. It's okay to not be able to do something in the conventional way. It doesn't mean your dream isn't achievable. I started writing music because this organization gave me the confidence to try.

How do you deal with awkward situations when you cannot understand someone or the communication breaks down?

I find myself in this position a lot, and for the longest time I did everything I could to not make it obvious that I didn't understand what was going on. I was afraid of making people feel uncomfortable. I eventually realized that it's best just to be honest. I don't like to be in a cab alone because I can't communicate sitting behind the driver. It's also a problem when the dentist has his mask on. Now I am honest about my limitations and try to work out a plan that will get us through whatever it is we're trying to accomplish. Sometimes the encounters are brief enough that I can just muddle through.

When you use an interpreter, should I talk to you or the interpreter?

If we are having a conversation, look at me and talk to me. The interpreters will tell me everything you say. I have such respect and admiration for people who have studied to become interpreters!

If you could pass on one piece of wisdom from your experiences, what would it be?

Don't confuse your dream with your identity. That way, if you fail at achieving your dream, it won't kill you. You are made up of so many dreams and talents, and failing is just the start of another opportunity.

Do you sing all the time at home?

Yes, I do. I tend to sing the song that is playing in my head, regardless of how many times I have sung it that day. It drives my poor husband insane because he has to hear one song on a loop, sometimes for days.

acknowledgments

Thank you from Mandy:

From the bottom of my heart I am thankful for the following people:

My mother, Valerie Harvey. For so much of my life, you have been the person who has been the driving force that kept me moving forward. When we, and I mean *we*, had to deal with so many surgeries, you assumed the role that was always needed. And that sometimes meant you had to be the bad guy and push me past what I thought was my breaking point; in those times, you always reminded me that I was so much stronger. I love you and I adore you, and there will never be enough words to say thank you.

My father, Joe Harvey. It is truly amazing to look back at how we started. Picking up the guitar as our way of communicating all the way to being as close as we are today. Thank you for being a mentor and partner in crime. Your knowledge and advice have shaped me in more ways than I am aware of. I can't wait to see what the future will hold, and the idea that you and Mom will be there with me makes me feel a rush of calm and excitement. Now let's go fishing!

Katie, Sammi, and Josh, my amazing siblings. Thank you for all of your patience and all of the laughter even throughout the dark times. I have the best family in the world, and you are a huge reason why that is true.

acknowledgments

Erik Weihenmayer, adventurer and No Barriers USA founder. Erik, I know I have told you this many times before, but you are the reason I started writing my own music. When we first met, you inspired me to look inside and evaluate my fears. No Barriers USA and you have taught me a new way to live and have changed the core of who I am. Erik, I am so excited for more adventures—even the horribly scary ones involving heights, or worse . . . the ocean!

Cynthia Vaughn, vocal coach and teacher. Cynthia, thank you for being such a dear friend through all of the many years we have known each other. Thank you for instilling in me a passion to work hard on music and to enjoy the work. You are dear to me, and I am so blessed to have you in my life. I am also so blessed for your sister, Chris Ann Bass. Chris Ann, you saw something in me long before most did, and I know you kept it a secret for a long time. Thank you for being my anonymous donor in helping me pay for private voice lessons.

Karl Kispert, my business partner and friend. Even though we just met two years ago, I feel like we have known each other our whole lives. Thank you for pushing me past my comfort zone and for being such a motivator. You are the best, T2!

Chuck Hurewitz, entertainment lawyer and pianist. Chuck, you are the reason this book was put together. Thank you for reaching out to me two years ago and for connecting me with such amazing people as well as being such a light in my life.

Charlotte Gusay, my literary agent. Thank you for believing in me and this project. You gave it life and helped me navigate this crazy world of writing books. Thank you also for your warmth and constant encouragement.

Ed Keane and Jason Marcil, my management/booking team and friends. Thank you for your continuous work and for your friendship. I am so excited to be on this journey together and that you are not only helping me improve my personal experiences with music but, hopefully, helping many others experience music in a different way.

acknowledgments

Adam Cave, my high school choir director. I know we haven't kept in touch, but I wanted you to know that your passion for music education is the reason I wanted to become a choir director. Your love for music and music theory is infectious and has been instrumental to my way of life now. I hope I get to see you in the future to be able to thank you in person.

My dear husband, Travis Meler. Gosh, I love you! Thank you for creating a world where I always feel loved. My life has been forever changed, and you are one of the driving forces behind that change. Thank you for loving me the way I am and for encouraging me to grow into a better version of myself. I can't wait to spend the rest of my life with you!

The Melers! Tom (aka Pom), Terry, and Dominic. Thank you for welcoming me into your lives and your family. I am so blessed to have you in my life and for us to grow together. Pom and Terry, you are the best in-laws a girl could ask for, and I hope you know how much I adore you.

To Mark Atteberry, cowriter and jazz lover. Mark, without you, this book would have never happened, but more important, I am so thankful for your friendship and your words of wisdom. Thank you for breathing life into this project and for changing me in the process. I am beyond blessed to know you and honored to call you my friend.

And lastly, to the many friends and family who were not specifically mentioned. Mainly because I ran out of time and this book would have been a million pages long had I kept going. You have shaped me into who I am today and made me into a better person. Lisa, Dean, Mara, Sean, Wayne, Kay, Isaac, Cathy, Meg, Travis, Sarah, Travis (very popular name), my grandparents, my extended family, and so many more. You have all been such a motivator in my life, and I can't imagine my world without you in it. On the days I was feeling beaten down, you were always there in person or in spirit, making sure I was not giving up. From the bottom of my heart . . . *thank you.*

acknowledgments

Thank you from Mark:

I am grateful to the following people:

My literary agent, Greg Johnson, of Wordserve Literary. Thank you for representing me with integrity and enthusiasm. And for helping us find clarity as we searched for the perfect way to introduce an amazing young woman to a world that will be better for knowing her.

Mandy's literary agent, Charlotte Gusay, of the Charlotte Gusay Literary Agency. Of all the contributions you made to this project, it was your cheerleading that meant the most to me. Everyone should have a person like you in their corner.

Mandy's father, Joe Harvey. You have an amazing gift for simplifying truth. Again and again, you came up with the perfect word or phrase when we knew what Mandy was trying to say but couldn't quite pin it down. Thank you for showing up at all those meetings.

Our editor, Philis Boultinghouse. Thirteen years after we met, I finally got to work with you. It was worth the wait. Your insights were spot-on, and I've decided you're a miracle worker because you actually made the editing process fun, which is something I would have said wasn't possible.

My wife, Marilyn. You never complain when I spend hours in my man cave pounding out words, or when I'm staring off into space as we're having dinner, or when I'm frantic to find a pen so I can write down a fleeting thought. You "get" that writers are a little different. Thank you for loving me unconditionally and embracing what I do.

And of course, Mandy. Making this journey with you has changed me. There are so many things I see differently now, so many things I understand that I didn't before. Thank you for that and for inviting me to be your writer. Now it's time for you to do for the rest of the world what you've already done for me. Wherever you go, whatever you do, just know that I will be somewhere watching and cheering and remembering with joy the many days we spent together creating this book.

notes

1 From a motivational plaque seen in a gift shop.
2 John Eldredge, *Desire* (Nashville, TN: Thomas Nelson, 2007), 97.
3 Anne Christian Buchanan and Debra Klingsporn, *100 Voices* (Bloomington, MN: Front Porch Books, 1999), 61.
4 C. S. Lewis, *A Grief Observed* (New York: Bantam, 1976), 42.
5 Allen Klein, *Winning Words* (New York: Portland House, 2002), 218.
6 Ibid.
7 *The Huffington Post*, March 28, 2013.
8 Carolyn McKinney, "Quotations," American Chesterton Society, www.Chesterton.org/quotations.
9 Mandy Hale, *The Single Woman* (Nashville, TN: Thomas Nelson, 2013).
10 James Emery White, *Embracing the Mysterious God* (Downer's Grove, IL: Intervarsity Press, 2003), 101.
11 "Positive Quotes," Positively Positive, www.positivelypositive.com/quotes.
12 Warren Wiersbe, *The Bumps Are What You Climb On* (Ada, MI: Baker Books, 1980), 9.
13 "Stanley Kubrick Quotes," BrainyQuote, www.brainyquote.com/quotes /quotes /s/stanleykub398563.html.
14 Neil T. Anderson, www.goodreads.com/author/quotes/24581.Neil_T_Anderson.
15 Glenn Van Ekeren, *Words for All Occasions* (Paramus, NJ: Prentice Hall, 1988), 349.

about the authors

Matt Salacuse/Devon Dey Reps

𝓜 andy Harvey is an award-winning singer, songwriter, and inspirational speaker with an invisible disability. Mandy lost her residual hearing at the age of eighteen while a freshman vocal major at Colorado State University. She tried pursuing multiple career options but eventually returned to music, her true passion. Though her hearing loss is profound, her timing and pitch are perfect and her passion is unmatched. She quickly became an in-demand performer and has released three full-length albums and an EP thus far.

She appeared on *America's Got Talent* in May 2017 and received the "Golden Buzzer" from Simon Cowell, which moved her straight to the live finals. In 2011, Mandy won VSA's International Young Soloists Award and lived a personal dream of performing at the Kennedy Center in DC. She also performs regularly at Dazzle Jazz Lounge in Denver, voted one of the top 100 jazz venues in the world. She continues to perform around the United States and has been featured on *CNN*, *NBC Nightly News*, BBC World Service, *Canada AM*, *The*

Steve Harvey Show, and in the *Los Angeles Times*. In addition to performing and speaking, Mandy is an ambassador for No Barriers USA, a nonprofit organization that provides transformative experiences for veterans, youth, and others with disabilities.

Paul Wasmund

Mark Atteberry is the award-winning author of twelve books, including *The Samson Syndrome* and *The Solomon Seduction*. He lives in Kissimmee, Florida, where his grandchildren's artwork adorns his workspace and reminds him every day how blessed he is. He can be reached at MarkAtteberry@aol.com.